SKETCH PEOPLE

STORIES ALONG THE WAY

T. J. BANKS

Inspiring Voices books may be ordered through
booksellers or by contacting:

Inspiring Voices
1663 Liberty Drive
Bloomington, IN 47403
www.inspiringvoices.com
1-(866) 697-5313

ISBN: 978-1-4624-0043-0(sc)
ISBN: 978-1-4624-0042-3 (e)

Library of Congress Control Number: 2011944675

Printed in the United States of America

Inspiring Voices rev. date: 01-09-2012

For Zeke, now and always—

The thing I'm able to do, I guess, is break down walls. If they think you're listening, they'll talk. It's more of a conversation than an interview.

—Studs Terkel

I think all those people I did stories about measured their own success by the joy their work was giving them.

—Charles Kuralt

So here is a pattern of people – a pattern woven in true colours with an extra strand of gold

—Muriel Grainger

Acknowledgements

With many thanks to Alina "Alex" Oswald, a star photographer and a great good friend. Alex, I couldn't have done without you.

AUTHOR'S NOTE

A history buff, I've always liked the work of Hans Holbein the Younger (c.1497-1543). Thanks to him, we have "images very lively" of Henry VIII and other major 16th-century players . . . likenesses so startlingly vivid, we almost expect the subjects to step out of their portraits and talk to us. And Holbein did not flatter: he painted what he saw, faulty lines and all.

What has all this got to do with *Sketch People?* Only that what I've tried to do here is create my own sketches, word-pictures that convey the essence of the people who've shared their stories with me. Nothing is re-touched, embellished, or in any way gussied up. All I've done is listen. My Sketch People speak for themselves.

Contents

Jay Amari

A ONE-MAN SHOW: JAY AMARI

TALKING WITH ACTOR AND writer Jay Amari is a whole lot like looking down a kaleidoscope. A turn of the tube or the conversation and the configurations of color and light tumble apart, shift, and re-form themselves. Twirl it again, and yet another pattern emerges.

What does remain clear and constant, however, is Amari's intense level of creative energy. He is the author of *Crosstown Traffic*, a collection of plays: two of them – "Cloudy All Day" and "The Greatest" – were finalists in the Actors Theatre of Louisville National Ten-Minute Play Series in 1992 and 1993. He has taught writing workshops at Columbia University. He has acted in film and on T. V., his most recent work being in "Manalive," a film based on the 1912 G. K. Chesterton novel. And he's working on several screenplays plus a story, which has been appearing in installments on Facebook.

So, a Renaissance man? Amari laughs. "I guess I am because I'm working on a self-produced film, shot on video, which is probably going to be different from any other kind of movie that anybody else has made." That movie, "My Day," basically covers "parts of a day, only it's

1

going to be four seasons, so there'll be summer, winter, spring, and fall. The film itself is going to be interspersed with archival footage from other films, which will add commentary to my daily activities." He'll also be weaving in a number of one-minute segments in which people tell him in a single sentence what *their* days are like. He has, he adds, scripted about 40 pages of it, "but now what I'm finding is, just the process of shooting is showing me all this other stuff that is available. [So it] has sort of become this process-oriented film. But I'm going to be very happy with it when I finally get it finished because you're gonna see a lot of growth in it. Documentary-like, but it's still a fiction film."

The other screenplay that he has been working on is definitely not fiction: "The Open Door" is based on *Operation Esther: Opening the Door for the Last Jews of Yemen* by Hayim Tawil and Pierre Goloubinoff. "That was a script that was a lot of fun to write," Amari reflects. "What makes it gripping is that early on in the book, you see that Americans in Yemen were being unfairly treated. I mean, they were being taken into custody without legal counsel; they were being cruelly treated—beaten, starved, tortured – and it's hard to understand why." What it came down to, he says, was that Yemen regarded the Americans there as Israeli spies. Thanks to Operation Esther, however, it finally became possible for Jews to travel out of the country "as long as they do not go to Israel. It doesn't mean that they can't eventually migrate to Israel – which many of them might do. But many of them went to Canada, which is neutral; some went to America. It's an interesting, interesting story."

His conversation is tremendously alive, whatever he's discussing . . . a refreshing mix of honesty and banter with flashes of self-mockery. "So, I'm in awe of *Crosstown Traffic*," he deadpans, holding up his book and hawking it to an imaginary audience. "I think it's well worth the $26.95 that it's available in, in hard copy. It's worth that—probably more." And a little later, he laughs at the thought of someone coming across the book on a used-book website years from now. "And they're going to say" – he pulls another voice out of his bag, quickly changing character – "Jay Amari? He owes me money. What happened to that guy? I'm gonna track him down.'"

Right now, though, Amari's talking about "Manalive," which has been re-set in the present. In the film, he plays Hawkins, "a minister in one of these churches where the lead character[, Innocent Smith,] comes." Basically, Smith "is walking across the United States, and he's spreading this philosophy about life and God, although God is never mentioned directly. With Chesterton, these ideas are very spiritually based."

Hawkins first appears in a mock courtroom scene: Smith is "on trial" for breaking into his own house, and the minister takes him to task for it. "My character's saying, 'Leave people alone. You're basically like an anarchist, so you *should* spend time in jail,'" Amari explains. Smith's "walking the globe like John the Baptist. He's going to touch as many lives as he can and get to the basis of these value systems, and that's the overall point of the film, as I see it." Hawkins is "not really driving a lot of the action. He was there to add ideas."

Granted, there's a certain static quality to the original story that they had to work around. "You have to be involved in the ideas to make it fly," he admits. "As an actor, you try to personalize it and make it objective because what is personal to you will show your emotional connection to an objective goal. An objective goal that represents idealistic needs of a character can be understood by anyone, so that the character can be seen dealing with ideas."

He takes this idea and spins it out a bit. "There's a very strong element in every actor's performance when he has to understand what drives a character, what a character believes. Sometimes even if a character disbelieves or doesn't believe in God, that can be the spiritual side of the character. Even the most evil character in the world has a spiritual side." Dramatic case in point: a doctor he played in "Forensic Files" who killed his wife: "Even though he was a surgeon who had helped thousands of people, he was still capable of committing murder, and he was positive that his decision was the best possible one for himself." Amari describes it as "one of those techniques that is part of the acting craft – as an actor portraying even the darkest of characters, one must be able to justify his character's actions on positive life-affirming reasons."

He approaches the writing and staging of his own plays in the same open, intuitive manner. "I would bring in the words, and the actors would bring in stuff that you would never imagine," Amari recalls. "That's what makes the collaborative effort so rich. You're not just working in a vacuum: there's another person coming in with a slew of ideas . . . . The actor will always show the writer something different from what he has in mind because the actor sees the end result and the writer sees the motivation. The actor will see a key line or a group of words that are really at the heart of what the character is doing to get what he wants . . . . That is ultimately what drama is about."

And yet for him, the spirit of his writing has remained intact. "In regards to hearing and seeing my plays performed," he observes at another point, "I cried at every performance, not really cried, but you know how it is when you hear your own words, especially shared with a room full of people you don't know. It feels like being in a sleep for a long time and then waking up to realize that everything before was an unpleasant dream – like understanding completely the emotion we call love. Ultimately for me, it feels like I have become a slightly better person."

The talk turns specifically to "The Owners," a play that Amari is currently adapting into a screenplay. Onstage, one of the main male characters, Bob, was actually played by a woman. "It worked amazingly well," Amari says. "There's this duality that comes into the play when you have a woman saying male-driven or masculine lines." It also shifted the play's focus from male-female relationships in general to empowerment.

Even without that twist, "The Owners" is still powerful stuff, thanks to some vivid imagery and moving speeches. Most of the latter come from Adam, a terminally ill gay man: "So I am dying, and I cannot share that thing with anyone because it is happening to me, and I have no words to describe what I feel. I'm stuck in the middle of it." Or, later to his sister, Katy: "I own this body, and I don't know what's going to be here because all I know is this is where I live, and I'm being evicted . . . they're turning off the water and electricity and letting the building go." There's a raw-boned honesty, a fierce yearning to those lines that grabs the viewer or the reader by the throat.

"With 'The Owners,' I wanted there to be moments when the characters would break," Amari explains. "They would have these moments where they could go into these long operatic pieces where they had a chance to do something with a monologue." Now that he's switching genres, "a lot of it's getting changed . . . . Dialogue in the movies is so tough. You really have to be a stylist – you have to have characters who come in and cut right to the quick."

This point came up a lot when he was teaching script-writing at Columbia. He had fiction writers come into his classes looking to write screenplays or stage plays. "They had characters talking like prose from a novel," Amari recalls. "And I'm going, 'No. You won't be able to get anyone to sit through this because characters come in when they want something: they come in to get it, and most of the time, the dialogue represents their trying to get what they want . . . . In soaps and other T. V. shows, you have characters who look at other characters and say, 'Why did you come here?'" He starts inventing dialogue as he goes along. "`Yeah, I came because you have my diary, and I'm not gonna let you blackmail me anymore. So, you either give it to me now, or I'm gonna shoot you.' Or courtroom scenes. It's the easiest way to get information out there."

One last turn of the kaleidoscope brings us to the story he has been running on Facebook. More about the process, really, than about the story itself. "It's funny, it's kind of great," Amari says with a laugh in his voice. "I have to read it aloud to myself – I guess it's probably my acting training. But I have to hear how the words are tumbling out." There are space limitations on Facebook, of course, but he has made those limitations work for him, "creat[ing] tension to drive the story . . . . As a writer, it forces you to condense words and meaning and produce a more intense experience for the reader."

"It's just a story now," Amari reflects. "But by the time I finish, it could be an exciting screenplay . . . . Writing is hard. I get up in the morning, and I say, 'Why am I doing this?' I *have* to do this." The same holds true in regard to his acting – a feeling that's summed up for him by a remark he once heard actor Harvey Keitel make at a workshop about there being "`two kinds of actors – those who want to act and those who need to act, and those who need to act are going to be doing it the rest of their lives.' And I guess that's what I consider all the time. The desire to be an actor supersedes any measure of success based on financial gain. Sometimes just making that decision to pursue some measure of success by means of a particular craft can be considered success."

Amari returns to this thought near the end of our talk, referencing the business manager in "Citizen Kane": "He has a great line. He says, 'You know, making a lot of money is not a difficult thing to do if all you want to do is make a lot of money.' And during the course of the film, you realize how making a lot of money-- if that's all you want to do—that's basically how you've defined your life. And at the end of your life, what do you have?"

Related links:

- http://www.imdb.com/name/nm1494875/
- http://www.lulu.com/product/paperback/crosstown-traffic/773432?productTrackingContext=center_search_results

EVERYTHING DOVETAILS: LOUISE E. JEFFERSON

(This is one from The Way-Back Files—an interview with Harlem Renaissance photographer Louise E. Jefferson, March 1984.)

****

"Everything dovetails, you know. You have no idea how many kinds of information, picked up one place or another, will come in handy . . . . A commercial artist must have an encyclopaedic mind – for you can never tell what you will be called on to depict or interpret."
-- Louise E. Jefferson in an interview with
***Opportunity** magazine, 1947*

****

Louise E. Jefferson is a hard lady to pin down. A talented graphic artist, illustrator and photographer, the first black person to ever do Voice of America, and a close friend of such Harlem Renaissance figures as sculptor Augusta Savage and poets Langston Hughes and Countee Cullen, she is oddly – and maddeningly – close-mouthed when she wants to be. She doesn't like to be questioned about dates, partly because she doesn't want people to know how old she is (one of her stand-by lines is that she must be older than 65 because she's retired) and partly because she prefers to think of things in "chunks of time" rather than in terms of actual dates. "Your mother," she says with infinite scorn during an interview at the home that she has shared with her enormous and beloved white cat since 1972, "must've been frightened by a calendar."

The Litchfield, Connecticut-based photographer doesn't always take kindly to questions about her work either. She likes to downplay it all, especially the illustrations. "I don't care much for illustrations," she says shortly.

Other people do care considerably, however. Jonathan Bruce, director of the Community Renewal Team (CRT) of Greater Hartford, Inc. Craftery Gallery, and James A. Miller, Associate Professor of English and Intercultural Studies at Trinity College, have put together an exhibit of those illustrations. The exhibit, which contains a large number of pieces from Jefferson's nook *The Decorative Arts of Africa* (The Viking Press, 1973), opened at the Craftery Gallery on Main Street on February 5 and will be running through March 30.

Jefferson, of course, makes her usual show of grumbling about the exhibit and everybody making her do it in the first place. She also spares a grumble or two for an upcoming exhibit of her photographs of Litchfield and New York. "I'm always busy," Jefferson says. "I mean, anything's work if you'd rather be doing something else." Whether anybody ever really makes her do anything is another question altogether and one that she laughs at when it's actually put to her. "Damn good question," she admits. "I'm embarrassed . . . . No, they sort of *goose* me into the deal. I like to think about what it is first – give it a good deal of thought."

Jefferson, who will be honored by the Connecticut Historical Society this year, is the recipient of numerous awards and honors. Her works have been shown at the Baltimore Museum of Art, the Schomburg Collection of the New York Public Library, the New York Bank for Savings, the Oliver Wolcott Library in Litchfield, and Trinity's Austin Arts Center. The illustrations in the Craftery exhibit have been selected from the cumulative results of her four trips to Africa between 1960 and 1972. (That first trip also led to Jefferson's being asked to do the Voice of America program on account of her being the only black person—actually one of the few people of *any* color—traveling there to celebrate Ghana's becoming a nation.)

"That's from a photograph I took," she says, glancing at an illustration of a 12-year-old Mangbetu tribe girl from northeastern Zaire. "You can't do a lot of sketching in Africa like that. You can take field notes now . . . . If I can sketch in a hurry, I bring field notes home, and then I have to write all over as to what I'm sketching so that I remember it when I do the finished work." Sometimes, she adds, it takes her two or three attempts before she manages to get it all down on paper the way she really saw it.

Jefferson started out in typography, which her father Paul (himself a calligrapher for the U. S. Treasury Department) gave her a few rudimentary lessons in, and then moved on to cartography and calligraphy – "all those 'phy's," as she puts it. She always loved drawing, and her father supplied her with all the paper she could possibly want. She trained herself as a photographer. She doesn't remember exactly when she started but claims that she turned out her first successful photograph in 1940, when she was visiting the Tuskegee Institute in Alabama.

The photograph—which Jefferson still has carefully tucked away in her files, even though she speaks disparagingly of it—shows a sad-eyed shabbily dressed boy who looks like he stumbled out of a Walker Evans shot. "Do you like it *that* much?" the photographer demands. The disbelief in her voice is very well done. "I wandered off the campus, trying to get the feel of Alabama, which I didn't much like. I was on a back road, and I heard this whimpering. And there was this little boy sitting on someone's steps, and I asked him what was wrong. He said, 'They won't give me a penny,' and he started crying all over again. I gave him a nickel, and that's when he really did cry." She laughs at the memory. "Gee whiz! A whole five-cent piece!"

She calls it her first real photograph because it was the first one she ever took that really *felt* like a photograph. "There's a difference between a photograph and a snapshot," she says, "and I *hate* snapshots. When I developed this and saw this, I said, 'That's not a snapshot, that's a photograph.'"

She begins rooting through her files, grumbling some more but throwing out a tantalizing comment or two along the way. Just enough to hook you. "You don't want to look at this stuff," Jefferson remarks casually.

It's worth being reeled in. There are photographs of Rosa Parks being finger-printed after her arrest; Eleanor

Roosevelt ("I took such good pictures of her," Jefferson remarks thoughtfully); Carl Rowan; Paul Robeson; Cab Calloway; and Louie Armstrong. She laughs at the shot of Calloway with his back to the camera. "That's his back*ground*," she hoots gently. She softens as she studies the Armstrong photograph, letting her genuine pride in it show for a second. "I still think I took the best picture of Louie Armstrong that's ever been taken."

On the walls of her workroom are a slew of photographs of Harlem Renaissance figures, some of them taken by Jefferson. She claims she came to New York in the early 1940s. Miller, the show's curator, differs with her on this point, however. He says that the names figuring in her stories—and the fact that the Harlem Renaissance had pretty much ended by 1940 – make it much more likely that she arrived in the city a decade earlier.

Jefferson'll give you two different reasons for her going to the city in the first place. One is that she figured she might as well see if she could make it as a photographer and an illustrator in New York because if she couldn't make it there, she wouldn't be able to anywhere. The other – which is, on the whole, the better story – is that she came to New York to visit friends, was robbed, and ended up staying rather than wiring home for money.

"I went to spend 10 days," she recalls laughingly. "I had just bought what I knew was the most beautiful raccoon coat in the world . . . . I put all the money I had in that pocket. Now, this particular day – it's in February, now – I decided to visit [activist and writer] Pauli [Murray, a good friend of hers,] to see what she was writing, and I'm in the street, showing off . . . leather jacket and about 45 cents in my pocket. I left the raccoon coat home with all the paper money in it." When she returned to her room to get some books for Murray, she found both coat and money gone. "I never went back home to live. I couldn't face the family."

Whichever story is true, Jefferson ended up staying in New York for at least 26 years, working as the art director of the Friendship Press (the publishing agent of the National Conferences of Churches) from 1942 to 1968. She studied graphic arts at Columbia University and fine arts at Hunter College but took degrees from neither. She worked in the Harlem Artists Guild with Savage, who was extremely active in the Work Projects Administration (WPA) in the 40s.

Savage was only one of the Harlem Renaissance figures whom Jefferson was friendly with. "You name 'em all, and I met 'em," she says. Langston Hughes was "a doll" and Countee Cullen somebody she felt "very close" to. She gets up to find some copies of Cullen's poems—which she herself bound in leather and which are inscribed "To Lou Jefferson, Cordially, Countee Cullen" – and a photo. "Here's a picture of Countee," Jefferson laughs, "on the lawn over there in a robe – he's just gotten up, and he's pretending he's playing golf. He couldn't tell you whether the ball was round or elliptical."

When pressed for actual stories about these folks, however, she balks, protesting that the ones she knows are already in the books. What she does like to reflect back on is "Harlem as such. It was safe, comfortable, clean . . . . Nothing like it today, nothing like it anywhere. The theaters were all doing well. There is no such thing as a theater in Harlem now, no such thing. There were fine stores on 125th Street, now which is a jungle – fine stores." Jefferson takes a drag on her cigarette. "There were four theaters on one block . . . . Night shows. It was a wonderful era."

And that's all she will tell you. You're left with all the bits and pieces and contradictions that make up Lou Jefferson and a strong sense that you haven't gotten even half her real story. "Just call it fiction," she says. She shrugs. "It's all fiction. Nobody's ever going to believe all the things that have happened to me."

REMEMBERING — AND LOVE — TACK

THERE IS AN IMPRESSIONISTIC quality to Pearl ("Tack") Tackett Cannon's watercolor landscapes. Light and shadow meet and merge; the outlines of houses, barns, and trees are a little wavery, and roads and paths suddenly fade away, leaving us in places that feel haunted by things we can't put a name to, let alone see. A few deft brushstrokes suggest trees twisting and dancing in the wind . . . snow scuttling across a field . . . or water moving, its moonstone shades shifting. The sky's grays, blues, and mauves are softly blurred, reflected onto the snow.

It's all part of what Tack called "the arrangement of things" – the way that patterns of line and color, light and shadow catch and hold your eye. "You'll be running along," Tack told me once, "and there'll be a scene." Tack was a trained artist, but she never messed with fancy terms when simple ones would do.

I met Tack when I was a child. Back then, I simply thought of her as the nicest person in my mother's rug-hooking group. I knew she painted – Mom had one of her paintings hanging over the sofa in the living room – but at 11, I didn't give it much thought.

We lost touch with Tack for awhile. Years later, as a young reporter for the local weekly, I was casting about for feature ideas, and Tack suddenly came to mind. My mother remembered hearing where she'd moved to: I called her, and the next thing I knew, we were visiting with Tack in her apartment off her daughter's house.

She was a good interviewee and could conjure up word-pictures almost as vivid as the landscapes she painted. At 86, she had experienced a wealth of history: she told us about the first motor-car she had ever seen ("Look, John!" her mother had exclaimed to Tack's father. "There's one of those things!") or the time her teacher had dismissed class early so that they could see the primitive plane that had landed near their one-room schoolhouse.

At some point during that first visit, she led us down to the cellar studio she shared with her daughter, a high-school art teacher. One watercolor – an unfrozen brook cutting past some trees in a snowy clearing—called to me strongly. I bought it for the grand sum of $25.

A few weeks later, the interview ran. The following Saturday, Tack called me. "You did an A-one job," she said in that soft Southwestern drawl of hers. "I want you to have the picture as a gift."

We began visiting on a regular basis. She'd tell me about growing up in Grapevine, Texas and the powerful need she'd had to draw, even as a small child. "When I was little," she explained, "we had no good paper to draw on – only rough paper and hard pencils you couldn't draw with." So she drew on anything that she could lay her artistic little paws on – the blank end pages of books or even the fine sand of the wash that ran through her father's alfalfa patch.

As she grew older, Tack did chores for the minister's wife in exchange for art lessons. "Some of her stuff was just copied," Tack recalled, "but she knew how to mix colors . . . . [so] I did her laundry [in order] to learn." She managed to pick up a few more lessons by winning a drawing contest in the local paper. Finally, one of her still lifes earned her an art scholarship at Baylor College for Women right before World War I. A supportive teacher arranged for Tack to sell her smaller paintings to other students for badly needed cash, and she washed dishes for room and board.

She shared these and other stories with me during our visits. She quickly became one of my best interviewees, and I worked in features about her whenever I could. I even broached the possibility of a book, only to learn that Tack's granddaughter had already spoken to her about doing that very same thing. The matter seemed pretty much closed.

That spring, however, I received the following note from Tack:

*Dear Tammy – Are you still interested in "the book"? If so, let me know – Lisa is **so** busy – that she **can't** do it! Right away, anyway.*

So – give me a call and we will talk about it – love – Tack.

So we talked about it. A lot. Something in me knew I wasn't ready to write that book yet; but I took plenty of notes and even tape-recorded some of our conversations for the day that I would be.

And, of course, there were the paintings. Tack never exhibited them, but she was always working on something. She sold me paintings for ridiculously low prices, even giving me one or two that she laughingly dismissed as "throwaway sketches." But, then, she was like that about her work, frequently bartering it for whatever small favors friends did for her. Money and publicity didn't matter to her, I learned – only the art.

And I was learning something else during those visits: the stories and paintings mattered less and less to me than Tack herself did. She had worked hard, she had suffered – her only son had been killed in World War II – and yet she'd come through it all with her spirit intact, no pun intended. She became an oasis, an understanding presence in those days when I was going to college and working two newspaper gigs in my attempt to earn my stripes as a writer.

"You have it in you, too," she murmured once, studying a quick sketch I'd done. Somehow I don't think she was talking as much about the sketch – my drawing skills are cartoon-ish and minimal—as she was about that creative spark burning in both of us.

She understood other things equally well. When my father died suddenly from a stroke, she sent me a note that simply said, *Remembering – and love – Tack.* As always, she'd gone straight to the heart of the matter.

Tack is long gone, of course. In one sense, that is. In another, she is always with me: her paintings hang in almost every room of my house, and that presence of hers lingers with me, as do her stories and what she taught me about art. I haven't written that book we talked about – yet – but she remains one of my best interviewees.

Goat Magic:
Nancy Butler & Lyric Hill Farm

S HE HAS GONE FROM being a geology major and a Master Gardener to living a totally corporate lifestyle to making and selling goat's-milk soap. This last incarnation is clearly her happiest. "I have goats! I live on a farm!" she chortles. "I learned to drive a tractor! I can milk a goat!"

That one short speech says a lot about how Butler tackles everything. Whole-heartedly. Thoroughly. Her business, Lyric Hill Farm in Granby, Connecticut, has been in operation for a little more than a year. But there were about six months of trial and error, she admits: "Of course, I couldn't do it the easy way and use somebody else's formula. I had to make up my own formula. I wanted certain qualities that certain other soaps didn't have – I didn't want to have exactly the same soap as every other goat-soap maker around."

The more you talk to her, the more you realize that all those disparate strands in her life aren't so disparate, after all. A geology major at Cornell University with a minor in civil engineering, Butler loved working with nature.

"Geology was in the engineering department and in the arts department," she explains. "Geology allowed me to spend time outdoors. Ithaca is a beautiful place. And I got to travel to lots of places to do fieldwork – Wyoming, Montana . . . . And it was absolutely beautiful."

She did her stint in the corporate world, working for 10 years as an environmental and safety engineer at The Travelers in Hartford, Connecticut. "It was kinda like OSHA [the Occupational Safety & Health Administration] from an insurance company's point of view," she explains. "I loved it – I was interested in how things were made."

And then there was her passion for plants. In 1995, Butler took a Master Gardener course, working as a garden advisor at the White Flower Farm in Litchfield and as a horticulturist at Westmoor Park in West Hartford. She and one of her friends at White Flower Farm were, she recalls, "such confirmed plantaholics, I knew we had reached an all-time low when I was holding her by her ankles while she was rooting, no pun intended or" – she looks up from the Belgian linen washcloth she's knitting, clearly re-thinking this – "intended, in the dumpster for plants. This arm comes out – she holds it [the plant] up and goes, 'Tree peonies!'" Butler laughs. "It was like the Holy Grail."

The goats butted their way into the picture later on, part of her son Austin's "4H project run amok." Lyric Hill Farm came about because they had a surplus of goat's milk: "My kids were getting sick of goat cheese, and they said, 'This has got to stop.'" Butler had always wanted to make soap, so she set up shop in the kitchenette off the front of their circa-1895 house. She prefers keeping the business small, she says, adding, "I don't ever want to have large batches because I like the feel of it being hand-made and not a mechanized process. I would rather have multiple small batches that I can make by hand than have a large vat done by machine." Butler has even begun knitting her own washcloths to sell along with the soap because she refuses to purchase cheap washcloths made in China "on account of their labor practices"; besides, she likes the rougher texture of the linen. And, of course, plant person that she is, she appreciates "the botanical connection. It comes from a plant[, flax,] so it kinda comes full circle."

But that botanical connection comes into play in more ways than that. "I am very committed and tied into the sustainability of plants and farming and keeping as low a carbon footprint as possible, at least in my everyday life," Butler maintains. As a cancer survivor, she is intensely concerned about what ingredients go into her soap. Not only does the milk come from the family goats, but the herbal infusions are from her own plants. She does use some "tried and true" essential oils, but everything is food-grade—excepting, of course, the lye, which is needed to saponify the oils and turn them into soap.

She even uses rain water off the roof to dissolve the lye rather than run the risk of possibly offsetting the process with minerals from well water. "I used to come home from work with my suits and my laptop," she laughs, "and here I am now with my buckets, getting rain off the roof."

But it has all come together for Butler. She talks frankly about her bout with cancer – "It shook my world" – but she doesn't allow it to define who she is. Her garden has helped with her healing. "I don't have to smell them or ingest them," she says regarding her flowers and herbs. "They're just lovely to look at. For me, working in the garden is very spiritual." And the goats have become part of that healing spell as well. "There's something very magical," Butler says thoughtfully, "about looking out on your pasture of goats, and the next day, you're milking them, and it's turning into milk for making soap, for making cheese."

Related links:

- http://www.lyrichilfarm.com/index.html

Ingrid King with Amber

HOOKED ON A FELINE:
INGRID KING & BUCKLEY'S STORY

BUCKLEY CAME TO INGRID King when she was working as the manager of the Middlebury Animal Hospital in Virginia. The tortoiseshell rescue with the bent leg wasn't the first cat to wander into the writer's life; but she packed an emotional and spiritual wallop that King has yet to recover from. Not that she wants to. "I didn't realize how much she [Buckley] opened my heart and changed my life until I was in the middle of the changes she brought about," King admits.

Buckley's Story (iUniverse, Inc.), winner of the 2010 Merial Human-Animal Bond Award and a National Book Awards finalist, is her tribute to her wise furry muse and mentor, the "little cat [who] was pure love." Think of it as a feline *Tuesdays with Morrie.* "Her freedom-loving spirit inspired me to finally make the leap of faith and work for myself," King says. "She taught me about letting go of fear and worry and to live in the moment. And finally, she taught me that sometimes loving means having to let go, no matter how painful it might be."

King had always had a strong spiritual kinship with animals; she had also always been keenly interested in Reiki, a form of energy medicine that dates back to early 20th-century Japan. A little more than a year after Buckley entered her life, the two passions came together for her. She left the veterinary clinic, bringing with Buckley with her, and opened Healing Hands, a home-based Reiki practice. She worked with animals and humans, often sending distance healing to both with powerful results. Her favorite distance-healing story involves a 15-year-old cat down in Florida. "She had virulent nasal discharge caused by calici virus, was not eating or drinking and was very frail and had very little energy," King recalls. "After just one distance Reiki session, this kitty started eating – in fact, she got up towards the end of the session and went to her food bowl and ate for the first time in days. She continued to improve with subsequent sessions."

Buckley, her "little Velcro cat," started out as official greeter to clients but quickly added assistant Reiki practitioner to her duties. She'd "jump up on the treatment table and curl up next to or on top of the client." It soon became clear to her owner that Buckley was positioning herself next to whichever part of the client's body needed an energy boost. Clients began reporting "a feeling of added heat or pulsing where she had been." After awhile, King just skipped sending Reiki to the areas that Buckley had already seen to.

Even in her day-to-day life, Buckley "radiated" a joyful healing energy, "transmut[ing] the energy of the house in general," King observes at one point in her book. "Cats are sensitive to energies and have the ability to change negative energies into something peaceful and calming . . . More people commented on the peaceful energy in my house after she came to live with us than ever before." Amber, the other tortie-in-residence, had "a quieter, more serene energy" of her own. "Between the two of them, they had the vibrational spectrum of aligning with Source covered," the writer reflects.

The word-picture that she paints of their lives together is lovingly detailed, the colors rich and warm. But the best memoirs, like Rembrandt's paintings, have a certain amount of sadness and shadow in them, offsetting the glowing hues, and *Buckley's Story* is no exception: Buckley, the little cat with the brave, beautiful soul, was suffering from heart disease.

King did everything she could, but she was finally forced to admit that she couldn't control the outcome. "For a recovering control freak like me, that was not an easy challenge to overcome!" she admits. "It was a gradual letting-go process, but it was probably accelerated by her because of the kind of cat she was." Buckley fought being pilled and acted up at the vets', thus closing off a number of possible life-prolonging treatments: "It was going to be her choice how far we would take treatment, and when she would be ready for transition." So King followed her lead, trying not to focus so much on treating the cat's illness "on a physical level." Instead, she "learned to really connect with her [Buckley] on that deeper level, and to honor both her wishes and my own intuition with regard to what was right for her."

Buckley lost her battle on November 28, 2008. One of the great strengths of the book is King's treatment of her beloved friend's death. She does this without morbidity or sentimentality, only with loving honesty. The shadows that creep into those last chapters only underscore the beauty of their camaraderie.

And, in the end, that is what we take away from *Buckley's Story* – that and the loving buoyant spirit of the cat who, like the teacher in the adage, showed up when the human was ready for her. King herself sums it up best. When asked what word-picture of Buckley she'd like to leave the reader with, the writer says simply, "Joy."

Related links:

- http://www.ingridking.com
- http://www.consciouscat.net

THE MESSAGE

THEIR LOVE OF DOGS had always been a strong bond between Ollie and Arvilla Allaire. "My mom and I were extremely close," Ollie says of her late mother, "and we've always had dogs." That closeness is an almost tangible thing, even now: talking of Arvilla, she has a tendency to slip into the present perfect tense, almost as though the former's just a room away. "She has always been an animal lover. So that was a big thing for the two of us. I can never remember a time in my life when there wasn't a dog in our household or more than one . . . . None of these dogs did we ever go looking for: they always found us."

Viking came to them courtesy of Mamie, an old family friend who was selling the inn she'd been running up in Chester, Massachusetts. When Ollie and her mom came up to help with the move, Mamie showed them a litter of puppies belonging to the folks who'd bought the inn. Each had been spoken for except for the pint-sized Viking.

"Mamie had fallen in love with him," Ollie remembers, "and said, 'I don't know who's going to take care of him now that I'm leaving.' And my mother says, 'Well, I don't think we're going to leave him.' So she picked him up, and he was just a little ball of fur."

Viking settled into his new home in Westfield, Massachusetts easily, becoming extremely attached to both Arvilla and Mamie. About the time he turned three, however, Ollie and her mom noticed that he'd frequently fall over while he was running around in the backyard . . . almost as though he was having a seizure. The vet checked him out and explained that because Viking "was such a hyperactive dog, he would eat so fast, then go outside and want to throw it up. But as it started to come up, it would cut off his wind, and he'd pass out." Once his throat relaxed enough for the food to go down, however, Viking would literally be up and running.

Arvilla took charge of the situation, heading out to the yard whenever she spied the dog acting up. She'd catch him and "kinda rub him underneath his stomach and say, 'C'mon, Vik, you know you can do this. Mom's right here – I'm going to help you through this.' And, sure enough, she did, and he wouldn't pass out. She'd get him to deal with whatever, and, finally, it became a little less and a little less. But he still did it."

Then Arvilla died of cancer in January 1984. "Vik, you can't do this anymore," Ollie told the dog. "I'm not Mom, and I can't do the same thing for you that she did."

Viking started losing weight. Special foods and formulas didn't help: soon he was losing three to five pounds a week and making the trip to the veterinary clinic almost as many times in the same week. Finally, her vet said, "I don't see it often, but I think this guy's dying of a broken heart." He told Ollie that she needed to seriously think about having the dog put down "because at this point, you're not doing him any justice to keep him."

So Ollie had Viking euthanized. Mamie, by this time, was living in a senior-citizen complex in Westfield. She had, Ollie knew, frequently dreamed about people who had died and had, in fact, had a few dreams about Arvilla since her passing. They hadn't been particularly significant dreams – just ones that had left her with a strong sense of her best friend's presence upon waking.

But the dream that came to Mamie after Viking's death was strikingly different, Ollie says, adding by way of explanation, "When Mamie had lived at our house, Viking used to go in and wake her up sometimes by putting his head on her bed. Just the hot air from his nose and his breath would wake her up, and she'd reach over and pet him and say, 'Good morning, Vik. Yes, I'm awake, and I'll get up.' Then he'd trot out of her room."

On this particular night, Mamie told Ollie, "I dreamt that Viking was next to the bed. I kinda looked down, and there was his little head looking up at me. When I did what I normally do – reached to pet him – I swore I felt fur, and I immediately woke up." And there was Viking sitting by the bed.

Mamie turned toward the doorway and saw Arvilla. "She never said a thing to Mamie," Ollie continues. "She just looked at Mamie and smiled, then said to Viking, 'O. K., Vik, it's time to go.' Viking trotted over to my mom, and that was it. They were gone."

"I couldn't believe it," Mamie told Ollie afterwards. "But I know that I saw those two plain as I'm talking to you right now."

Mamie never dreamt of Arvilla again. But to this day, Ollie doesn't question the story. "Maybe it was a sign that he was with her, and they were both fine, and that was it. They gave us the message."

A Living Craft: John & Dorothy Kalahan
Of Illuminations

I T STARTED WITH A broken lantern outside their house,
Dorothy Kalahan says. She and her husband John
"went to a stained-glass store. We thought we'd buy some
glass and have them cut it for us so that it would fit.
And we looked around and said, "This is pretty – we can
do it.' So, before we left, we had signed up for lessons."
And they "actually did make little panels to put into that
lamp . . . eventually."

The lamp was left behind when they moved – it was a
stationary one – but the lessons stuck. Their business,
Illuminations Glass and Custom Engraving in Bristol,
Connecticut, has been going strong for 21 years. The
technology has changed, of course. In the beginning,
explains Dorothy, their designs called for carbon paper,
paper, cardboard, "and wiring things with the carbon-
paper drawing around it so that I had more than one cut
out. Then we had a pattern to work with." Now they just
do the designs on the computer and print them out to
the size they want.

But that's not the only change. She used to carry a notebook with her and take "copious notes. When I took photos with the film camera, it would be like 'Writing, writing, writing – picture #1 was of this. And picture #2 was of this, and, oh, I hope that picture comes out.'" Now she carries a digital camera with her "in case some really cute dog walks by or something." She does some Photoshopping but only if the photo's too dark for her to make out the lines of her subject. Then she has to "lighten it up. I don't care if it's centered. I don't care if it's a bit blurry. I just have to see the strong lines of an item – the major lines – to do a design."

Both Dorothy and John agree that their pieces have improved. Not only are they better constructed, but they also hold together better. She does most of the design work, and he does "the majority of the physical labor" – i.e., the glass-cutting and –grinding and soldering. But there's definitely some overlap. John, who has worked for both Pocket Books (he sold Harlequins) and the phone company before he retired, comes up with a lot of the ideas. Dorothy, who has a full-time job in a medical library, will put the foil on the pieces while she's watching T. V. at night. "The foil goes on the edges," she explains, "and then you put the glass back together like it's a jigsaw puzzle, and you solder it."

They do commissions. One of their most challenging ones was a stained-glass window commissioned by the University of Connecticut Health Center's Class of 2004 as a gift for the facility in Farmington. "I said, 'O. K., what do you want in it?'" Dorothy recalls. "And they said, 'Oh, I don't know. Something to signify medicine, dentistry . . . maybe research.' I said, 'Well, let's see. Medicine – a caduceus is a really nice symbol for medicine . . . .'" A little more brainstorming, and they had the design down: a caduceus, a cross-section of a tooth ("So that there would be more detail than just a blob of white," Dorothy observes.), and an old-fashioned microscope.

Most of their designs are taken from nature, reflecting their appreciation of animals, birds, butterflies, and various flora. A Red Abyssinian cat, her eyes glowing yellow-gold. Two river otters, one resting its paw over the other's shoulder. A deer entering a clearing. A wolf howling at the moon. Several owl designs, including one of a barred owl, its wings outstretched.

There are back stories to many of these pieces, and John shares some of them. He points out some of the differences between the wolf and deer designs. "What we did there," he says, "was that we created a painting, except that what we do is [more] like a line drawing. We simplify. We have the glass do the work. With the wolf, there's a lot of moisture, there's foliage, and there's reflections. We selected a glass that had a hint of green throughout the blue of the night sky.

"When we look at the doe," he continues, "she is coming out into the glade in the fall: it's cold, and the air is dry. And that is reflected in the glass around also. There's no reflection from any foliage – there's no greenery – it's just the cold fall sky. She sees something, and it reflects her environment." So they not only created "the look of the doe" – they also created the look of the world around her.

It is, he insists, "a living craft. Doing glass, you can see" – he pauses reflectively – "things change. The light will change." Case in point: a flower design he was working on once. "It had a little green and yellow or blue or something. And I got a hold of some pieces of glass where the colors merged. I mean, it was beautiful. And for the life of me, I can't figure out what happened because I've used glass from the same manufacturer since then, trying to get the look, and I've never been able to." It's almost as though the piece, like a character in a book or on a T. V. show, took on a life of its own. "You become the agent. We make up the stories. And we try to make the things . . . become."

He moves on to one of the owl pieces . . . based, as it so happens, on an owl they saw at a raptor show in New York. "Dorothy took his picture," John recalls. "The poor fellow didn't have the moon that night, so we created one for him." It is "a layered piece. The fat part is a white glass with some clarity to it: we filled it in the back, but the brightest part is where the moon would be. I left that open, and what happens is, it disperses light just like real moonlight would."

Sometimes it's a matter of creating a context – of leaving things out to give the work dimension, as with the owl piece. Other times, it's a matter of altering the existing context slightly, as John learned from a plastic thermometer in his grandfather's tobacco weighing shed many years ago. The thermometer was, he says emphatically, "the ugliest thing I had ever seen in my life. I said, 'Why would you get that?' He [the grandfather] takes it off the wall and holds it up against the light." And then John saw the way the light filtered through that junky old piece of plastic, transforming it. The effect was, he says, very similar to that of stage lights coming through a scrim. "And something like this" – he gestures toward the stained-glass piece – "it's a little like a stage, too."

The Kalahans may not have trained as artists per se, but they know their craft inside-out. That's partly because they do all the design work themselves, Dorothy maintains. "Most people don't. But because I've taught myself to do it, I can see things that need to be there to bring out the animal's personality, for instance."

The other part of it – the major lines of it, as she herself might say - is that the need to create is an almost tangible thing in both of them. "Dorothy and I have always valued creativity more than anything else," John observes. "I mean, there's stuff you just *do*" – he chuckles – "and there are things you create. The latter make things better for others, and you get a lot of satisfaction from doing it."

Bernadette Kazmarski

Renaissance Woman with a Feline Twist: Bernadette Kazmarski

I know that depth was invested in the portrait itself, showing in a physical manner – I always say that I paint until my subjects look back at me – and perhaps in a spiritual manner as well, recognizable by both humans and animals.

—Bernadette Kazmarski

****

SHE DIDN'T REALLY DRAW in college, Bernadette Kazmarski says. Oh, she took the required beginner's art courses, but she was seldom satisfied with the results. "Every once in awhile, I'd hit it," the Pennsylvania-based artist and writer recalls, "but I wasn't consistent. I know now it was there in me, but I needed to let go. I was being too logical – 'I have to draw this line this way. Look how she drew that line.'" So, when she graduated Edinboro State College, it was with an English literature degree, not with an art degree. "I specifically changed my major from art to writing because I was afraid I wouldn't get a good enough grade."

After briefly doing public relations work for a mall, Kazmarski got a job as a typesetter, which "got me into graphic design." She was still doing her artwork, but she wasn't really feeling like artist.

Then came Sally, a deaf white Turkish Angora in need of a home. Kazmarski had always had cats, many of them fosters, and it was only natural that they found their way into her art. But this was different. She was working from photos of Sally, and the process of tracing them on a light table (a box with a glass top and lights in it, "something like a slide viewer, only bigger") helped her "keep everything in perspective, literally and figuratively." She was using rag watercolor paper, and she "just felt the surface and said, 'I can draw on this. I like this.' It was an intuitive decision."

Drawing Sally "totally awakened my visual skill," Kazmarski insists. She had always been a highly visual person – "I think in pictures all the time" – but she had needed to get out of her own way. And that was exactly what happened during "that process, and when I finished that I realized why I couldn't draw before . . . . It's not what you produce – it's what you see and what you do with what you see." She had transcended the technical aspects of her craft: she had "visualized the finished work, and actually created what I had visualized. This is what has to happen for anything I render, whether it's a commissioned portrait from photographs or a drawing *en plein air* [French for "in plain air" – a technical term for drawing from life]."

She had a similar epiphany while working on "After Dinner Nap," her pastel rendering of another beloved cat, Stanley. "I looked at the way I handled light, color, and composition, and I was astonished by what I had done . . . . It's actually going beyond the logical mind and just letting it happen."

All the elements in her work – paintings, sketches, block prints, photographs – fall together of their own accord, as though Kazmarski has simply channeled them. She is there, yet she is not there, and it is that wonderful contradiction that makes for the magic in each piece. That and the quality of light. You expect a sensitivity to light in artists and photographers, yes; but Kazmarski takes it up a few notches. She uses light the way poets use the rhythm of words. She leans toward Impressionism in that respect. "With the Impressionists, it was all about how the light fell on things, which is certainly how I paint," she muses. "All sorts of light bounces around in a scene, and their goal was to bring out the color they saw." It's a good description of what Kazmarski does.

Her writing has that same textured feeling that her art has. She has a knack for painting word-pictures that draw you in, and nowhere is this more evident than in her blog "The Creative Cat." It is actually only one of five blogs that Kazmarski does. But it's the one in which her writing and artistic talents come together right elegantly.

Which is interesting because blogging was one of those happenstance things for Kazmarski: it found her at a Cat Writers' Association (CWA) conference back in 2007. She had just won the group's Muse Medallion and the Hartz Everyday Chewable Vitamin Award for her article "Loving Care for Your Older Cat." She "was really surprised," admits Kazmarski, who had been focusing mostly on art and graphic design at that point. "Sometimes things will happen that will guide you." She went to the conference, and "everybody was talking about blogging. That's when I decided rather than work with my clunky old website,

I would use my website to display finished work and the blogging for works-in-progress."

And so "The Creative Cat" was born. Kazmarski plays with the blog, much as she plays with light in her artwork. Sometimes the post will be a discussion of what she's currently working on ("The Portrait"). Sometimes it's a photo followed by a few reflections ("Muted Colors"). And sometimes it's a personal essay about the cats in her life, past and present ("Cookie & Me, Our 18th Anniversary," told from Cookie's point of view).

As Kazmarski sees it, the blog has "become—and I don't know if this was intentional – a reflection of who I am." It allows her to write about whatever happens to be on her mind, or in her heart, at the moment: her garden, wildlife (her backyard has been a registered wildlife habitat since 2003, and she has been maintaining it as such for 20 years), animal rights, the local library, and, of course, her cats.

She wrote about her beloved Namir at the end of July 2009; then, about a month later, she was moved to write about him as well as about several other felines she had lost. Namir had been diagnosed with congestive heart failure in 2005, the same year that Hurricane Katrina hit; by the time he died in 2009, "a lot of things with Hurricane Katrina had been resolved." So, in Kazmarski's mind, there was a parallel between what the hurricane had done and what she had gone through with Namir and the five other cats – Moses, Cream, Sophie, Stanley, and Lucy—who had died in that nearly four-year period. The result was the poignant and powerful blog post "Perhaps the storm is finally over."

"When a situation presents itself, we never know how it will play itself out," Kazmarski says, "and that's true of the animals we take into our lives." Response to both posts was strong, and she became aware of how important an outlet the blog was for her.

What's more, "The Creative Cat" has allowed her to weave together her twin passions, writing and art. "I always wanted to be a writer," Kazmarski muses, "and I figured I would eventually find my way to being an artist. But I always thought you had to be one or the other." Then she discovered comparative arts – "combining two or more fields into one project or using all"—and she realized that it didn't have to be an art-or-writing thing. That she could do both, weaving them together, as she does in her recently released *Great Rescues* (Beauty of a Moment Publishing), a 16-month calendar that is a truly wonderful hybrid – part almanac, part illuminated Book of Hours—combining exquisite watercolor and pastel "portraits of rescued cats and their stories" with feline facts, quotes, and resources.

As we near the end of our conversation, Kazmarski tells me how she once thought about getting a PhD in comparative arts and teaching at the college level. That never happened. But she more than absorbed the idea of living as "a creative person rather than as an artist." And that is what comes through in her talk. She is acutely alive not only to the nuances in her art and writing but also to the need to use both to live whole-heartedly. Spiritually, even. "So I didn't get there academically," Kazmarski reflects. "I got there through life experience."

Related links:

— http://portraitsofanimals.wordpress.com
— http://bernadettsmarketplace.wordpress.com

Mark Remaly

A Hands-On Philosopher: Mark Remaly

His FINGERS MOVE OVER the woven chair seat like a fiddler's over his instrument. Only, in Mark Remaly's case, he's coaxing forth not music but story. "I don't consciously think about it," explains the caner, who owns The Seat Weaver in Westfield, Massachusetts with his wife, Alice Flyte. "But if I run my hands over a chair, I get the feel of it." Just the day before, for instance, a customer brought a chair into the shop: his hands came across some "dings" in its back, and he guessed that "a grandmother or somebody had pushed it into a sewing-machine for years and years, and she [the customer] said, 'You know, I think you're right about that.'" Something in the chair spoke to him, Remaly says, telling him or "releasing" its story.

That's a pretty common occurrence for Remaly, who has been working his craft since he was 15. Born with limited vision, he attended Perkins Institute for the Blind in Watertown, Massachusetts, and it was in a class there that he learned chair-caning. He discovered that he truly enjoyed working with his hands. "It's kinda like *re*-making," he reflects. "I don't think of it as art per se because I'm really just following what I've been told – y'know, over, under, over, under. But somehow it becomes more than just a bunch of cane. It becomes – hmm-m, what's the word I'm looking for?—a whole. It becomes strong enough to sit on, it becomes art, it becomes a craft. That's the thing I think I enjoy most about it: transforming a bundle into something practical, useful, & pretty."

Enjoy is a word that's very much at home in Remaly's conversation, snuggling into this sentence or that. He enjoys the rhythm of the work itself. He enjoys talking with the customers and helping them get "re-connected with their chairs." And, most of all, he just plain enjoys his life. The fact that he went completely blind eight or nine years ago hasn't curtailed his enjoyment. Granted, Remaly has had to find "different ways of getting information that I used to be getting through my eyes." He has "always been more of a hands-on person than a cerebral intellectual," he says, and the loss of his sight hasn't changed that: if anything, it has fine-tuned his sense of touch to the point where he really is able to pick up on a piece of furniture's smallest detail – the story in the wood, if you will.

The same holds true for other aspects of his life. He accepts that "we live in a visual world . . . that 80-plus percent of what people take in is visual. But that doesn't mean if you don't see, you miss 80%. There's something" – he sighs, but it's a reflective sigh, not a sad one – "that compensates. Touch. And when I say, 'Touch,' I mean the air moving by your face when someone moves their hand. To me, that's touch as well as tactile touching. Or the power goes off: you're looking to get out of the room, and you feel the wall before you actually encounter it . . . . I knew an English guy, and he used to snap his fingers all the time" – Remaly, getting lost in the story, mimics the gesture – "and get echoes off of buildings and this and that."

He gets a little blasé about his craft at times, Remaly admits. Then someone comes along and reminds him how unique what he's doing is "and how much they appreciate it. And that's a wonderful feeling because sometimes I'm thinking about other things while I'm working, or I'm coming into a difficult part that requires more concentration. It's never drudgery, but sometimes it gets put in the background until someone reminds me of what I'm doing[, and it's] 'Yeah, you're right, this is unique.' And quite often I hear, `I couldn't do that,' and that's not true. You have to, first of all, *want* to."

For someone who insists he's not cerebral, Remaly can do some pretty sustained philosophical riffs, especially when it comes to his craft. We talk about how there's a craving in many of us for texture and how a liking for old-time crafts, such as caning, pottery, and quilting, comes out of this feeling. "There's the enjoyment of the finished product," he reflects, "but there's also the enjoyment of just doing it." Caning is something he'd do "even if money weren't involved . . . . I get into a state when I'm caning: my hands are busy, [but] my mind is *half*-busy and has a chance to wander."

This is a man in love – with his craft, with his wife, with pretty much everything around him. He has learned to get past his blindness. And in doing so, he has become intensely aware of all the so-called commonplace things he might've overlooked before. He has *not* let his blindness be "the end of all existence.

"I just celebrated my 60th birthday in April," Remaly continues. "I've never been in a better spot. I really, really enjoy my life. If someone had told me years ago that at 60, my sight would be gone [with] no chance of it coming back – [that] I've accepted it, embraced it, and moved on, I wouldn't have believed it. I have a wonderful wife, my life partner. I see people all the time at the Y here whom I'm sometimes lucky enough to bring a smile to. There's no doom and gloom in my life. I wouldn't trade places with anybody, I'm thrilled to be me. So, that's how I feel right now, and I don't expect it to change."

PAINTING – & WRITING – WITH LIGHT: ALINA OSWALD

WRITING IS HER FIRST love, Alina Oswald says, although she's finding photography "another way to express what I want to say, another way of looking at things . . . . Every time I spend too much time in the photography part of life," she admits, "I start missing writing. It's a weird feeling[, y]et I love both of them, writing AND photography, I think, in different ways."

Still, the roots of that first love go very deep. Oswald, the author of *Infinite Lights: 9/11/2001 – 9/11/2011*, *Vampire Fantasies: A Collection of Vampire Photography*, *Journeys Through Darkness*, *Soul Cities*, *Backbone*, *Poetry of the Soul*, *The Awakening* . . . , and *The Best of MJ*, began writing when she came to this country from Romania in 1991. At that point, she was, she says, simply "jotting down my (very) raw thoughts on paper"; but by 2002, she'd published her first piece, "Dark Hour Friend," on ivyvine.org. Soon she was freelancing for a number of publications, the most prominent being *Art & Understanding (A & U) --America's AIDS Magazine*. A &

U dealt with HIV/AIDS-related issues, and that struck a chord with Oswald, who'd been radicalized by an AIDS conference she'd attended with her physician mother in Bucharest back in 1986.

Oswald's first assignment for *A & U* was a feature interview with AIDS activist and writer Joel Rothschild (*Hope: A Story of Triumph* and *Signals: An Inspiring Story*) in October 2003. Their paths had, in a sense, been running parallel for a long time. Rothschild had been diagnosed with AIDS in April1986, just a few days before Oswald had attended the Bucharest conference; by the time of their interview, he had outlived the death sentence that his doctor had handed him by almost 17 years. And he'd done it by sheer faith and determination, "scratch[ing] the surface of the Divine" and undergoing a profound spiritual metamorphosis in the process. He shared all of that with Oswald now as they talked.

She came away from their meeting transformed. When her husband, Dirk, met her back at the hotel, she recalls, "I hug him and give him a kiss. It's not that I didn't mean it before[, but] after having this experience with Joel, I realized you have to hang on to something more while you have it because it's all temporary. You treasure every moment." She notes how her friends with HIV/AIDS "don't hang up on you without saying, 'I love you.' Joel's the same way – he doesn't leave home without patting his dogs and telling them how much they mean to him. And he does the same thing with his friends . . . . He was the first HIV-infected person I ever stood with. I was just in awe of him, and I still am." Rothschild, she adds, "opened my eyes to another kind of world."

The interview was the first of many powerful pieces that Oswald would write for *A & U*; it was also the beginning of her involvement with the LGBT (lesbian, gay, bisexual, and transgender) community. "It's impossible to write about HIV/AIDS and not get involved in the LGBT community," she observes, "because the LGBT publications are the only ones that cover AIDS. Whenever have you seen anything about AIDS in *Woman's Day* unless it's about 'Rent' or those books and movies that connect more with the mainstream?"

No one would ever have branded Oswald's stories "mainstream." She interviewed Ntare Mwine, a photographer, playwright, and actor who had written a one-man show called "Biro" about an HIV-positive Ugandan who enters the U. S. illegally, seeking treatment. (The article became hcr first cover story for *A &U.)* She wrote about African-American women married to men "on the Down Low" – i.e., gay and very much in the closet. About hemophiliacs who had been infected with AIDS and/or hepatitis C through blood transfusions and "who had their houses set on fire . . . . Some of them got kicked out of their houses and towns and had to travel to other places literally and start from scratch where people didn't know them." She might not have a journalism degree, but she had something much more important – the ability to become totally engaged with whatever topic she was working on.

"It's funny," Oswald muses, "because my husband was reading my articles in the beginning, and he would say, 'You like this guy,' 'This guy you didn't really connect too well or too much with,' or" – she laughs – "'This sounds fine, but there's no soul in there.' But I usually connect with people or review a book that I like." And she definitely connected with Rothschild and other "kindred souls" in the LGBT community. Or, as she puts it, "You talk to them, and you forget to take notes. As a writer, you are in awe. And they really change your perspective in life."

She became a vastly different kind of writer. "I used to write a lot about death and being more dead than alive" – Oswald laughs at her old self – "and after I met Joel, I began writing more about AIDS." More than a few of the pieces in her first book, *Poetry of the Soul*, deal not only with the disease but also with Rothschild's "tale of triumph,/Healing and forgiveness/ . . . Of hope." And *Journeys Through Darkness*, her biography of fellow photographer Kurt Weston, is a tale of another kind of triumph: though now legally blind from AIDS, the award-winning Weston continues to work – or, as Oswald puts it, to use "his life experience to create art that is dynamic, informing, and also transforming."

What makes all of this so interesting, of course, is that Oswald is a straight woman working in a non-straight community. She has become, in her own words, "an adoptive member" of that community. "I don't consider myself as part of the mainstream," she says earnestly. "For a long time, I've been struggling with this idea that society says you should be this way, and you're this way, and society is trying to change you. Now I'm at a point in my life where I'm more comfortable with the way that I am. I am crazy – I'm unconventional – I'm not mainstream. So what? Why I like to work with people from this community is that they don't try to change you. They adopt you."

All this doesn't mean that she writes only about AIDS and the LGBT community, however. Her latest books, *Infinite Lights* and *Vampire Fantasies,* are definite departures from her earlier work. *Infinite Lights* is, as its subtitle indicates, a collection of photographs related to 9/11. Oswald and her husband were living in Massachusetts in 2001, but they happened to be visiting New York City the Sunday before the attacks. They even "stood at the footprint of the Towers. And then we went back home. I went to teach – I was teaching then – and then it happened."

Since moving to New Jersey, she has made a point of photographing the Tribute Lights each year. For her, they are a reminder that "we are still capable of kindness, understanding, unity, compassion and patriotism, as we were in the aftermath of the 9/11 attacks. One day that reminds us of all we've lost . . . of those who have given their lives trying to save others." Her photo of the Katyn Memorial – a bronze soldier with his hands bound and a bayoneted rifle in his back – in Jersey City calls to mind the Expressionistic work of artist and sculptor Kathe Kollwitz (1867 – 1945); and the shot of the lights across the Hudson River conveys a sense of both physical and spiritual illumination. "The back-stabbed soldier and the 9/11 lights in the background have something in common, I think," Oswald observes. "In both cases, the enemy back-stabbed the victims . . . . [They] never saw it coming."

By contrast, the photos in *Vampire Fantasies* reflect our curious love affair with those beings who have no reflection. Oswald, who jokes about having "a vampire accent," believes that the living dead fascinate us because "they are beautiful. They live forever. They have superhuman powers. For some reason, this vampire character keeps re-appearing in some other shape or form. The vampire from *Dracula* is not the same as the vampires from *Twilight*." And while she thinks we're "pretty much over the peak of the vampire craze," there is, she adds, "a truth of some sort lurking behind the legends . . . something that we are subconsciously drawn to and that she would like to further explore in "some sort of collection of pictures about the background theory about all these vampire stories."

Photography has become an increasingly important part of Oswald's life. In a sense, this second love of hers grew out of her first: when she was writing for *A & U*, she quickly learned that "if you didn't have the pics, it was no deal." So, in order to keep her stories from being killed, she began shooting her own photos. By 2008, she was taking photography classes at B & H in New York City. "I love it," Oswald enthuses. "The topics that I photograph are the ones I follow. I have a dark dramatic side of me, and I have a colorful side . . . . With black-and-white photos, it's painting with light." Literally – after all, as she points out, "photo" means "light" and "graphy," "drawing."

Actually, "light" is a word that comes up frequently in her conversation. She uses it mostly in regard to her photography, of course: she frequently works with a flashlight to achieve the effects she desires, "the smaller, the better. You can be more precise and paint the details better." But there's an interplay of light and darkness in Oswald's writing, too. In much of it, she is chasing the shadows with a metaphorical flashlight, "cover[ing] the non-mainstream subjects – maybe the forgotten stories or the disregarded ones, but I'm fascinated by them and love what I'm doing with all my heart."

Related links:

— http://www.alina-arts.com

DREAMING IN ROMANIAN

(From The Way-Back Files – <u>Woman and Earth</u>, March 1996.)

I AM STANDING IN THE center of the room, staring up at a woman who seems very tall to my four-year-old eyes. She has thick white hair, glasses, and a navy-blue dress with white polka dots. My father is standing behind me in his work clothes. They are talking; but now, when I try to re-enter that memory-picture, I cannot hear her voice. It's as though someone has pressed the mute button.

It is my first memory and the only one I have of my Romanian grandmother. And, even though I didn't know and love her as I did my maternal grandmother, she somehow took hold of my imagination. Her Romanian-ness fascinated me. It was colorful, exotic, and mysterious. All the other Jewish kids I knew were of Russian or Polish descent; and there was no other family member alive to tell me what my Grandma Dena's homeland had been like. Later, when I grew up and began to write stories loosely based on her life, I went into research mode, pulling together what bits of information I could find. But there didn't seem to be much about Romanian

Jews: the only book I managed to lay my hands on was Michael Gold's *Jews Without Money* (1930), and the picture he sketched of his father's Romania was . . . well, sketchy.

Then, too, there was a curious feeling of disenfranchisement. This was my experience, and yet it wasn't. Romania hadn't, from what I could gather, treated her Jews much better than Russia had . . . although, as poet and Chicory Blue Press founder Sondra Zeidenstein (herself of Romanian Jewish descent) said, they seemed to have had more of a cultural life than the Russian Jews had had. Still, I had the sense that I imagined my grandmother had had – of being of the country yet not of the country. Of belonging yet not belonging.

Perhaps in Romania it is easy to have this feeling because there are so many different influences at work and no clear definition of what Romanian really is. Originally part of the Roman Empire, it is, as Hannelore Hahn, the President of the International Women's Writing Guild (IWWG), points out, "the only country in Eastern Europe that speaks a Romance language. And its major influences on its educational system have been the classics and French culture." To the west, in and around Transylvania, which once belonged to the Austro-Hungarian Empire, there's a heavy Hungarian influence; to the north, in Moldavia, the culture and traditions tend to lean more toward Russian-Ukrainian. And the southern part of the country, once a possession of the Ottoman Empire, shows a definite Turkish influence. A Gypsy counterculture (for want of a better word) also exists, although that probably isn't as strong as it was prior to World War II.

Of that other perennial counterculture, the Jewish one, little remains. Interestingly enough, though, most of the Jews who originally settled in Romania were *Sephardic* (a term that basically means "Spanish" but that refers to any Jew who follows *Sephardic* liturgy and traditions) Jews from Spain, Turkey and the Balkans: documents show Spanish Jews living in Walachia as early as 1496, courtesy of the Inquisition. The *Ashkenazi* (German-speaking Jews) came later. More undercurrents. The country that my grandmother left as a child of 12 in 1896 was a melting pot in which none of these diverse nationalities ever really melted.

It has remained a place of paradoxes, especially for women. Hahn, who traveled there this past May, recalls how an American professor told her, "The women of Romania are alive . . . . [T]hey work often at two jobs, they take care of their children and everything else. Not so the men. Their spirits are broken." Hahn herself perceived a feminist spark in the universities, where the department heads were men who needed female professors to translate for them because they themselves knew no English.

But it's also a country that has been brutal to women. Under dictator Nicolae Ceausescu, the mandatory pregnancy policy led to many women dying from coat-hanger abortions. "And if you got caught having an abortion or using some type of birth control," says Angela Green, a 27-year-old Romanian woman who has lived in the U. S. for the last nine years, "you would be in prison for a long time. And if you were to go to a doctor because you had an infection from an abortion, or you were bleeding, the doctor wouldn't treat you unless you signed a paper saying what you had done."

Green has that same sense of belonging/not-belonging that I have, even though she isn't Jewish. The country she left behind is still very much "a man's country" with "a man's religion" in her opinion. "The man's up here," she says emphatically. "The woman's all low at the bottom. In any discipline you look at, it's the same way – family, religion, education, careers." Back in Romania, she would not have had the kind of career she has here, "although there are some women who go to medical school and a few who are good chemists." Most of the poets, composers/songwriters, and the like are male, she says: she knows of a few female singers, "but where the creativity comes in and the things that women could actually be doing, I mean, I don't see too many women." Craftwork does provide a creative outlet of sorts for "the farm women in the villages in the winter," Green adds, "because there is no farming [then]. They make their own clothes, they make rugs – you name it, they make it. In the village, everything is hand-made, and the woman is the one who is doing that."

It's not much of an outlet, but it's something. And that's more than Romanian women have in other respects. Few drive. Domestic violence is very common. There are no agencies for battered women to turn to: the only shelter they can hope for is with their families, which may not be all that much help. "I think the majority of women are being abused physically and emotionally by their men," maintains Green. "It's a way of life, I guess, and they accept it for what it is. I've seen it around my mother, my father, both sides of my grandparents, my aunts, my uncles, neighbors, friends." She tells me how the village priest asked her maternal grandmother if she forgave her abusive husband when he was dying. The old woman, who "had a lot of scars both on her heart and on her body," shot back, "No! Let God forgive him!" Green says she's glad to be married to an American man: "I find myself fortunate because I could have ended up with an abusive man . . . a controlling man."

The status quo of Romanian women at present is akin to that of American women in the late 19th and early 20th centuries with some vital differences: there are no feminist literary journals to express themselves in, no strong women's networks pushing for change. As Green sees it, the networking has to evolve in Romania, not here, to be truly effective. And she doesn't know a lot of Romanian women in this country who are willing to go back to help get that evolution started.

"Education is the most important thing," maintains Green. "If you give women the freedom to go and educate themselves – to go to college and learn what they can be – I think a lot of things will be changing. So the opportunity to educate, to have different positions and jobs other than being a housewife and a farm woman is the most important thing." Under Ceausescu, such opportunities just didn't exist, she says; and the system hasn't really changed since the same people are still in power. They no longer call each other "Comrade," of course. But the basic mindset is still the same, as is the attitude toward women; and it will, she thinks, take a couple of generations to change both.

Green herself can't escape that sense of being caught between worlds. Most of her family is, after all, still in Romania. "I'm young – I'll probably make a new family. But it will never be the type of family I would have if I had stayed there. I find myself, I'm losing the tradition. I'm losing a lot of the customs. And I'm actually losing the skill to write and speak the language. I used to dream in Romanian language. I don't do that anymore." There was, she adds, a transition period when she dreamt in both Romanian and English. Now she just dreams in English.

I find myself, I'm losing the tradition. Without realizing it perhaps, Green has voiced the dilemma facing Romanian women who have left their homeland: namely, that in order to find themselves as individuals, they've had to lose or let go of a tradition that no longer serves them. The trick for Green and her countrywomen is to craft a culture of their own – a new "family," if you will – using the best of what they've brought with them. To learn to dream in both Romanian and English.

CHICORY-BLUE WOMAN: SONDRA ZEIDENSTEIN

(From The Way-Back Files – <u>Poets & Writers</u>,
July-Aug. 1996.)

In northern countries only few wild plants flower in
November, but the gradually drying stems of the chicory
plant persist even in cold winters. The piercing blue flowers
appear from late spring right through to late autumn and
the strong, deep roots and the flat leaf rosettes protect
the plant through the winter. No wonder the chicory was
the symbol of perseverance and endless waiting . . . . The
growth of chicory on roadsides was regarded as a symbol
of its magic.

-- Riklef Kandeler & Wolfram R. Ullrich
****

POET AND PUBLISHER SONDRA Zeidenstein knows
firsthand about the difficulty of coming to writing
later in life. She didn't begin writing poetry until she was
in her late 40s and only then as the result of therapy and
a writing workshop that she was taking with poet Honor
Moore. "'OK,' I said, 'I will sit down and write for a year

and see where I am,'" she recalls. "When Honor seemed amused that one year could reveal much of anything, I said, 'OK, five years. Then, if I can't do that, I'll do something that's been in the back of my mind and that I know I can do: I'll start a small press and publish others' writing.'"

Zeidenstein made good on her word and, in 1987, started Chicory Blue Press, a feminist press, in rural Goshen, Connecticut. She named it for the wildflower that grows in the field at the corner of her street, a plant that appealed to her because of its "very pure, strong blue flower that opens only in the sun and closes at night."

The first book published by her press, *A Wider Giving: Women Writing After a Long Silence,* is a collection of poetry, fiction, and essays by 12 women who started their writing careers after 45. First published in 1988, the book is now in its third printing. "*A Wider Giving* came out of my own experience," explains Zeidenstein, now 62, "as well as a publisher looking for her first book to publish and finding it in the experience of being a late-developing writer."

Chicory Blue Press followed up with *Memoir* (1988), a collection of poems by Moore, and *Heart of the Flower: Poems for the Sensuous Gardener* (1991), which dealt with Zeidenstein's "other great passion – gardening." The press has also published a series of chapbooks by women writers over 60. "I'm looking for older women who are writing and who are looking for another publishing opportunity," Zeidenstein explains. Despite the differences in styles and genres among the writers published so far, "they all have an accumulation of years and issues [that] come from having been around a long time and having a lot to think about."

The first chapbook in the series, Zeidenstein's own *Late Afternoon Woman,* appeared in December 1991. Since then, the press has published six others: Carrie Allen McCray's *Piece of Time* (1993), Tema Nason's *Full Moon* (1993), Rita Kiefer's *Unveiling* (1993), Estelle Leontief's *Sellie and Dee: A Friendship* (1993), Anneliese Wagner's *Murderous Music* (1993), and Carol Lee Sanchez's *she)poems* (1995). Alvia Golden's *Acts of Love* is in production, and a chapbook of poetry by Nellie Wong is forthcoming.

All of the chapbooks have a similar format. The poetry or fiction is followed by a five- to eight-page afterword in which the woman "talks about what's on her mind as a writer." Zeidenstein debated for some time about whether to let the work stand by itself, then decided that she wanted the authors' personal voices to come into play "after the creative writing has been read and experienced . . . . What I wanted was to reach the readers of literature, of course, but also people who are writing so that they can be stimulated, supported, encouraged, or get ideas from the writers." Once she has, say, seven or eight chapbooks out, Zeidenstein intends to put them all together in an anthology format – a weaving together of genres very similar to *A Wider Giving.*

So far, so good. The response to the chapbooks has been "encouraging." Two of the books have gone into second printings, and almost all of them have been reviewed in such publications as *Poet, Brookline Citizen,* and *The Women's Times.* McCray's *Piece of Time* inspired an entire page of reflections on older women as role models in Gloria Steinem's *Moving Beyond Words* (Simon

& Schuster, 1994). "Even though this is a small print run and, at the moment, chapbook [format], I think that each of the writers is finding an audience and the work is getting out in a way that it wasn't before," reflects Zeidenstein. "So, that is very satisfying to me."

It's all the more satisfying because of what she has long seen as a trend in literature: the underrepresentation of older women's voices. Although she doesn't have any hard evidence for her belief that commercial publishers are less committed to working with 60- or 70-year-old writers as opposed to up-and-coming 20-year-old ones, she's pretty damn sure this is the case. "Look at any anthology or listing of books being published," she insists. "The ratio of older female writers being published to young writers of either sex or even to older male writers is quite skewed."

Part of the problem, of course, has to do with female writers stopping for long periods of time to raise children. But readers still need to hear these particular voices. Especially women readers. "We women enter our older years without having heard from older women what life looks like to them, what their perspective is," says Zeidenstein. "It doesn't matter that they write about age or not, but that they write as older and old women. If we don't have those voices in our literature, it's as if the cycle in life or the continuity of the generations is broken, and we have a very unrealistic or fragmented experience. And we need the history, we need the voices."

Zeidenstein's network is primarily European-American at present: only one chapbook author, McCray, is African-American. She has been reaching out to Native American, Latino, and Asian-American women writers because she has been "very excited" by their work. For her, "it's not a matter of being politically correct. It's a matter of wanting some of this writing because it's meant so much to me as a poet."

Ultimately, though, what Zeidenstein's looking for is "recent writing that is also the writer's strongest writing. I'm also looking for what I call strong, emotionally honest writing. The words can be very simple – they can be the most common words – but if they come from the writer's authentic feelings, they carry tremendous power.

"The press has found its niche," she continues. "I see myself, for the near and far future, as doing chapbooks. And though I say I'm looking for writing by women past 60, in my heart of hearts, I'm reaching for women in their 80s – if I can find them."

Related link:

■ http://www.chicorybluepress.com

Present Laughter: Maggie Hall LeVine

I T'S ALL IN HER expression, in the way she talks to folks in the audience as though they're friends she's sitting down to coffee with. Receptionist by day, stand-up comic by night, New Yorker Maggie Hall LeVine has a down-to-earth style that works well for her, both onstage and in her blog, "Maggie's Musings." "Hey, I like yapping about myself," she observes. "Why shouldn't I make it my life's work?"

Technically speaking, LeVine started doing comedy in the fall of 2006. But, in a very real sense, she has been doing it most of her life . . . if, as she remarks in that fast-paced way of hers, "you want to call being in seventh grade and wearing clothes that didn't match and wearing too much make-up because I didn't know how to wear make-up funny. People laughed at me then, but it was unintentional. Now it's intentional."

She acted for a few years, doing some television, indie shorts, dinner musicals, and off-off-Broadway plays. Then she landed a part in George S. Kaufman and Moss Hart's "You Can't Take It With You" as Alice, the one normal person in "a family of whack jobs. Even though she was the straight one, you have to have a sense of humor. And, ironically, my next major role was the comic relief in a murder mystery[, 'A Murder Is Announced']. I liked it – I felt more natural. And I knew that I preferred doing comedy to doing Shakespeare."

A life coach seconded that emotion, advising her to do stand-up comedy: "She thought it would be a good thing for me." So LeVine started combing craigslist for gigs. She landed a lot of "bringer shows" – i.e., shows that she could do as long as she brought five people to each performance. "It's very commonplace for new talent to bring in some audience," says LeVine, adding that doing this is "sort of like your entry fee."

In the fall of 2007, she began "barking," which basically meant going out into Times Square to pull in her audience. She now barks three nights a week, which enables her to perform the same number of nights that week. "Every so often, we have a chance to audition with Al, the owner of the Broadway Comedy Club and the New York Comedy Club," LeVine explains. "He sits down and talks with you about how you can improve. Even if he doesn't pass you, he doesn't make you feel bad about it." These are only two of the nine clubs that she performs at regularly. She also interns at the New York Comedy Club, seating people and making sure they don't leave without paying. She earns an extra spot during the week for doing that.

Some of LeVine's favorite bits involve telling long stories, "but you might lose the audience, so I don't do that too often. I tend to do personal stuff. I try to stay away from sex jokes because people can only take so many. I try to stay away from topical jokes . . . . When the audience is laughing, you know that they get you – or that they're roaring drunk."

She definitely prefers stand-up comedy to acting. "The other barkers or performers are like family," she observes. "Yeah, I think that's what we are. There's too much competition in acting – maybe three of you auditioning for one role – whereas in comedy, people are very supportive." To underscore her point, she tells about a fellow comic who'd been barking for four or five years before he was "passed" and could "get extra spots during the week without having to do extra work for it. That's a major goal for most comics starting out – to get stage time based on being funny, as opposed to how many people they bring . . . . We were all very happy for him. He'd been working very hard."

It has been tough. Once, three years ago, she got shot down in 10 seconds after spending all night in the street, waiting to audition for "Last Comic Standing." But LeVine, like Simon & Garfunkel's fighter, still remains. "It's like a lifestyle," she muses. "Y'know, I don't think I ever had a conversation with another comic that didn't involve comedy. We don't talk about family. We don't talk about the weather. It's `I'm doing this club.' Or, `I'm doing a spot.'" Eventually, LeVine wants to perform full-time. She's that determined. Or, as she puts it, "I guess comedy is one of those things where it's harder to quit than to keep going."

Related links:

- http://www.myspace.com/maggielevine
- http://facebook.com/maggielevine
- http://twitter.com/MaggieLeVine
- http://maggielevine.wordpress.com/
- www.youtube.com/maggielevinecomedy

BOBBIE'S EARRINGS

(This is a little off the beaten path for "Sketch People"
– but, then, so was Bobbie. In a world of pretty faces, she
was, to paraphrase the late Jimmy Durante, an original.
So here's to you, Bobbie, wherever you are. – TJB)

M Y MOTHER-IN-LAW'S EARRINGS ARE long and dangly.
The tops are deep-purple beaded triangles with
tiny white-and-purple hexagonal designs and black
edges: loops of silver, white, and purple beads cascade
down from those edges. They are colorful, exotic, sassy,
opinionated, and totally "boss."

They are very much like my mother-in-law. Bobbie, like
my husband Tim, was strong medicine: you couldn't ignore
either of them. They both had that "in-your-face" quality
and could and would verbally flay anyone they thought
a fool in twenty words or less. Actually, Bobbie could
probably have done it without even taking the cigarette
out of her mouth. Bobbie, I once told a mutual friend,
would never stab anyone in the back: no, she'd come at
him/her right up front, driving a tank and firing.

She was definitely exotic, favoring colorful Indian-
print fabrics, long earrings, and longer scarves. She loved

Oriental art (the only business trips she ever accompanied my father-in-law, Bob, on were the ones to San Francisco so that she could scope out Chinatown) and tigers (she had tigers—painted, china, and toy—parading all around her house, and all of them were named). She had a playful sense of humor, naming her over-sized fuzzy slippers with the koala-bear faces "Simon & Simon" after the then-popular detective show.

We didn't always agree with each other—sometimes we were irritated or downright angry with each other—but I always knew where I stood with her; and when she left a room, it was as if someone had turned the color down on a T. V. set.

We respected each other. She had been a reporter herself at one time; and while Tim and I were still dating, she secured me my first reporting job with *The Farmington Valley Herald,* the local weekly that she was an ad rep for. She was always interested in what I was working on, saying once to the room in general (she had a theatrical manner at times), "Tamathy"—her pet nickname for me—"is the only writer I know who gets paid for what she does." She was ready to listen during the slow times, when the only light in the proverbial tunnel was a flickering little match that I was holding up by myself. "I'm a good in-between person, Tam," she assured me with that light-up-the-room smile of hers. And she was.

But there was another side to Bobbie, I learned. For most of her life, she had battled with manic depression, having several nervous breakdowns. I never witnessed them—they'd occurred long before I appeared on the scene—but Tim described them to me in detail. With lithium and that particular brand of toughness that was her trademark, however, she finally learned to keep her demons at bay.

There's a scene in the "Anne Boleyn" episode of *The Six Wives of Henry VIII* in which the condemned Anne, still holding out for her daughter Elizabeth's rights, says to the archbishop, "I fight, Cranmer. For that is what I am made of. Fighting." Those words could have been written for Bobbie. For when grief came to her, she wrestled with it, just as she had with her mental illness. The night that Tim's van hydroplaned into a phone pole, killing him instantly, she and Bob came to me directly so that I wouldn't have to learn the news from some impersonal stranger in a uniform. She told it to me straight, not letting herself cry until she'd gotten the words out. Then she quickly got a hold of herself and sat down to make a list of things that had to be done.

It was, I think, her only way of bringing order to a world that had gone suddenly, terribly, heartbreakingly wrong. Tim had been her youngest . . . her "changeling," as she used to call him, although, in reality, they'd been so much alike, it had sometimes been hard to tell where one left off and the other began.

"I'm tough," she told one of my friends offering condolences after the graveside service. The "I can take it" was implied if not said. And in the year-and-a-half that remained to her, I only saw that toughness crack a few times. Once was shortly after the accident: the company that Tim had worked for met with me at the house to discuss the benefits package. Bobbie and Bob were there, too.

Now I had a few things that I needed to say to Tim's manager about some of the company's policies, which, I believed, had contributed to the accident. Bobbie knew what I was planning to say—was, indeed, more than ready to cheer me on—and was seated at the table, waiting. I stood behind her and, placing my hands on her shoulders for confidence, threw my rock into the company pond. In the silence that followed, Bobbie grabbed hold of my right hand and buried her face against it. But not a sound came out of her.

There was another crack on the New Year's Day after the tragedy. Bobbie had come over to watch a video with my three-and-a-half-year-old daughter, Marissa. I went upstairs to get a book I wanted to show my mother-in-law. Coming back down, I caught a glimpse of the hungry, utterly bereft look on Bobbie's face as she held Tim's child on her lap. I closed the book and stole quietly away, knowing that Marissa was doing all that anyone could do to ease that terrible ache in her grandmother's heart.

Fighting might have been what Bobbie was made of, but even she couldn't defeat the cancer that ravaged her body like wildfire. Within two weeks, she was gone. But somehow she has never really felt gone to me—in a large part, I suppose, because Marissa has grown up to be very like her "Grammie," both in looks and personality. She even has Bobbie's singing voice.

But there's more to it than that. Bobbie was definitely a personality to be reckoned with. A friend of mine who knew her from her ad-rep days with the *Herald* remembered her coming into the store where he was working "with her fur coat and clipboard. She never asked you what you wanted—she told you what you needed."

The fur coat was fake, but the attitude was real. So, on days when I'm feeling a little unsure of my next step—or need to metaphorically place my hands on someone's shoulders while I'm taking it—I don my sassy earrings. The Force—or, rather, The Bobbie—is with me.

From Birds to Big Cats:
Tippi Hedren & Shambala

(This interview first appeared in <u>Just Cats!</u>, Jan./Feb. 2001 as part of my "Making a Difference . . . . " column.)

AS ACTRESS AND ANIMAL-RIGHTS activist Tippi Hedren sees it, "My modeling career and my entire acting career were all a stepping-stone to this." "This" refers to her work at Shambala, the big-cat refuge that she started in Acton, California back in 1981. It is, she adds simply, "the most important thing in the world to me."

She doesn't dwell much on either of those previous lives of hers but admits that her roles in movies like "The Birds" and "Marnie" have given her "a sort of window. A person who has celebrity is able to call attention to certain causes." She finds it interesting that three of the actresses who worked with director Alfred Hitchcock – Kim Novak, Doris Day, and herself – have gone on to champion various animal causes. "I don't know," Hedren muses. "Is it because of the honesty of the animals? I don't want to bad-mouth Hollywood, but Hollywood can be very hurtful. Animals are very honest, and it's a wonderful thing to know an animal. I love all animals, but getting to know a wild animal is fascinating."

And she has had plenty of opportunities to be fascinated. Shambala, which officially became a wild-animal preserve in June 1983, thanks to the establishment of The ROAR Foundation ("Actually, we were a preserve before we knew we were one," Hedren comments with some amusement.), is home not only to lions and tigers but also to cougars, leopards, a jungle cat, snow leopards, a Florida panther, an elephant, several servals, a cheetah, a bobcat, and a liger. The latter, Patrick, is the result of a happenstance romance between a lion and a tigress. "He's very, very beautiful," the actress says of the hybrid cat. "He seems to have the best qualities of both."

Patrick wasn't born at Shambala – he came there courtesy of a small zoo – but many years ago, a tigon (a cross between a tiger and a lioness) was. They don't buy or trade animals and haven't bred any since 1981, Hedren explains, but "we had a birth like this at Shambala because we had two tigers who weren't getting along, and when they fight, they will fight to the kill." One of the malcontents was put in with some of the lionesses: it turned out that one of them was in season, and the tiger "was only too happy to oblige." Ergo, the tigon.

As her conversation quickly reveals, Hedren has developed an ever-deepening love and understanding of the wild cats at Shambala (which, in ancient Sanskrit, means "A meeting place of peace and Harmony for all beings, Animal and Human"). "They're all absolutely, totally different in personalities," she enthuses. But that enthusiasm doesn't blind her to the facts. "Wild animals can't be tamed, and I can attest to that. So can my entire family." It disturbs her that far too many lions and tigers "are being kept in people's backyards without proper facilities. Keeping these animals in 8x10 cages – that is cruel and unusual punishment. Most states don't have laws regarding the keeping of these big cats[, and] more often, it's more difficult to get a dog license than it is to have a lion or a tiger in your backyard."

And the results can go way beyond frightening, as Hedren's files on accidents involving these "pets" show. A 4-year-old boy in Texas ("Texas is one of the worst offenders," the actress says.) had his arm ripped off by a big cat: fortunately, the arm was retrieved in enough time for doctors to be able to successfully stitch it back on. A female guide at an animal park in Colorado wasn't so lucky. While trying to show visitors how easy a particular tiger was to handle, the animal tore off her arm and ate it.

"It is horrifying," Hedren admits after recounting these tales. "And it's never the animal's fault . . . . The wild cat is really an insidious animal. They have a great capacity for love – a sense of humor – and they have their dominancy and insecurity problems. And in a split second, they can kill you."

Some of the smaller wild cats can be almost as tricky to handle. Tabby, the bobcat-in-residence at Shambala, is too temperamental for anyone to go near. And the servals have "a very strange personality. They can be quite nasty. They are now one of the 'in' exotic pets because they're small. They have these long legs, and they can do these karate chops, and they're very fast. I've only known one serval who maybe you could pet: she jumped up and bit me on the mouth, and that's the nicest one I've met."

Knowing all this doesn't dim her love and appreciation for these animals, "all of [whom] have their purpose." Asked if she has any favorites among the wild cats of Shambala, Hedren replies, "That's like asking a mother who her favorite child is. I had a tiger I was very close to . . . and I had a lion I was very close to . . . . Each animal is a unique experience."

Related links:

- http://www.shambala.org

A Modern Herbalist: Sara Thornton

S ARA THORNTON CAN TELL you how to make two different kinds of wine from woodruff; how coltsfoot helps colds; and how boneset, despite its name, was used *not* for setting bones but for treating fevers. She knows that bloodroot, like digitalis, is beneficial in small amounts, lethal in large ones. That echinacea, if taken "too long [and] steadily . . . will basically turn your immune system off, and you'll come down with the next cold that comes round the pike." She is well-read and sells herbal supplements, teas, lotions, and the like at her Ravenswood Natural Health store in Simsbury, Connecticut. She has a feline compadre named Flash, and a few hundred years ago, she probably would've been executed for witchcraft because of all of this.

But this lady's definitely not for burning. Thornton's approach to herbs is not mystical but hands-on and very practical. She draws on centuries of Western herbalism and can discuss famous herbalists like John Gerard (1545 – 1611/12), Nicholas Culpepper (1616 – 1654), and Maud Grieve (1858 – 1941) and their works in such detail, you would swear that she has talked shop personally with each in his or her turn.

Chalk it up to a lifetime of voracious reading and a very inquiring mind. Thornton had asthma as a child: at the time, she says, "the only treatment was to give an adult-sized dose of speed to the kid, throw you into some type of steam room – usually the bathroom – and you'd sit there for awhile. You'd be basically high on speed for a week, running around with absolutely no sleep and scaring the hell out of the neighbors." All that excess energy had to go somewhere, and it found an outlet in reading. Bored with books "about Dick, Jane, Spot, and Fluffy," she began devouring her older brothers' and sisters' books. "When you're 6-years-old and you're starting to read John Steinbeck" – her voice starts off matter-of-factly, but laughter soon overtakes her – "you know there's a problem." History – and medical practices throughout the centuries in particular—drew her, and, with "one thing tumbling into another," she was soon reading about comfrey-root poultices and various other herbs that the Crusaders brought back from the Middle East.

That was part of how it all began. The other part was simply that her parents moved around a lot: growing up, she ended up living in some pretty rural areas, towns that "still had these amazingly backwoods backwards opinions of anything that was female. If you were taken to the doctor at all, it was always 'Oh, honey, you really just need to get married and have a couple of kids, and you'll be perfectly fine.' It was very difficult to find a doctor who wasn't dismissive of anything that was wrong with a woman."

So Thornton started looking for self-cures and ended up making "a pretty solid leap to herbs when I was a teenager." She found that she had an instinctive feel for it. Friends and relatives "would come along and say, 'Hey, Sara, have you found an ointment for sunburn? I don't have any aloe.' Or, 'The baby has colic – what would you suggest?' 'Well, a little chamomile tea.' . . . I realized that Western medicine wasn't the be-all end-all and didn't have the entire answer for every single thing. That I could keep myself pretty darn healthy without having to go to the doctor every time I sneezed."

At college, it was pretty much the same scenario: the staff at the medical center there showed the same misogyny that Thornton had been all too familiar with growing up. "They were treating women as though they were full of hysteria rather than [having] influenza, sprained ankles, whatever," she recalls. "So, if I had a new injury, I would look for some alternative treatment rather than running off to the local doctor. Again, it was more out of necessity than anything else." And once again, friends came to her for herbal teas and remedies for their sports injuries and menstrual cramps.

Then "what seemed to be this really weird bronchitis thing" hit the campus. The center actually stopped dispensing medicine and sent students to Thornton instead, making her an herbal practitioner by default, as it were.

"By complete default!" Thornton laughingly agrees. "I went right over to the health center, and I said, 'Wait a sec – you told me last year that I was practicing medicine without a license and you were going to have me arrested. And I was doing nothing of the sort! I simply had my own herbs for my own use, my friends would show up, I would give them a cup of tea, and that was it!'" When she questioned the staff about their sudden change in attitude, their response was "Well, we can't do anything for it, and we know that you keep putting people on their feet."

After graduating college, Thornton rented an apartment from a retired English couple. She was, she recalls, "wildcrafting my own herbs for my cold mix – mullein, coltsfoot, red clover among them – and had hung the bunches to dry in an unused closet." Her landlords, Paul and Joy, dropped by one weekend to take care of a leaky faucet. Opening the drying closet to shut off the water, the older woman found the bundles of herbs and coldly assumed the worse. Thornton explained that they were part of her cold remedy: Joy "broke into this RADIANT grin and shouted, 'Oh, Paul, did you hear? Sara's a WITCH!' Paul toddled around the corner, peered at me through his glasses, and just beamed . . . . They were so delighted that their tenant was a witch, they dined out on it for a long time."

So, in a sense, what Thornton is doing at Ravenswood now is what she has always been doing – listening to people and trying to point them to the right ointment, balm, or supplement. If she has a counterpart anywhere, it is Mrs. Todd, "the learned herbalist" from Sarah Orne Jewett's *The Country of the Pointed Firs*—that "ardent lover of herbs, both wild and tame," who dispenses her remedies to the good folks of Dunnet Landing and who holds her own with the village doctor.

"I moved away from being doctor-centric" – Thornton laughs – "really, really early. It's not that I feel they can't do something good, but I don't feel they can do as much as they want or as much as they profess." She allows herself one "slightly jaundiced comment": "When they stop *practicing* medicine and they get it right, then I'll go to the doctor more. Because if they're practicing medicine, then they still haven't gotten it right."

Related links:

■ www.ravenswoodnaturalhealth.com

Joanne
Vallee
Brunelle

Pushing the Abstract:
Joanne Vallee Brunelle

S HE HADN'T ORIGINALLY INTENDED to become an artist, Joanne Vallee Brunelle admits. "I wanted more of the art education angle, thinking that it would be an easy deal. Well, it ended up being a double major, more like creating my own major." Finding it tough enough to finish her art major requirements in four years, she gave up on "the whole education angle, which I'm pretty glad I did."

Moving toward abstract painting was a gradual process for the Granville, Massachusetts-based artist. She started off "doing a lot of real natural forms, as all college students do – you draw what you know. I went to UConn at Storrs[, Connecticut], and I was surrounded by beautiful countryside, drawing cows and rolling hills and apple orchards and all of that traditional stuff. Still lifes and plants – things that are in your dorm or apartment." But after awhile, Brunelle grew bored with traditional subjects and wanted to move in a new direction with her art. She began "blowing up" objects, creating what she calls "macroscopic" renderings. So, instead of painting a pile of leaves, she would paint "one giant leaf, a single leaf all by itself, or leaves overlapping but from an exploded type of view. And it kind of brought it into a different plane."

Oddly enough, Brunelle wasn't familiar with Georgia O'Keefe's paintings at the time. Once she got a gander at O'Keefe's "giant kinds of flowers and giant jack-in-the-pulpits and different plants," however, she recognized an artistic kindred spirit. The discovery excited her: "I thought, 'O. K., I'm on to something here – what I'm doing is valid.'"

She began "stretching reality" in her work. She still painted landscapes occasionally, but she was much more taken with abstract art. "I wanted to do something that nobody else had done before," explains Brunelle, "so I kept trying to push that and find my niche. But in modern art, so many things have already been done, it was kind of hard to find something that was completely unique on the face of the earth."

Along the way, Brunelle took up picture-framing "because it was arts-related. It was like 'Oh, I'll be framing art all day—I'll stay in the art world.'" Today, she owns and runs J. Vallee Brunelle Fine Art & Framing in Granby, Connecticut. It has, among other things, allowed her to provide a place for local artists to meet and show their works.

"We had a little workshop yesterday for some of the Granby artists," she remarks. "Yesterday, it was my turn to host, and I picked the topic of 'Let's talk about abstract art' because I'm the only person [in the group] who does that kind of work." Some of the other artists even tried their hand at abstract drawing, "and some who had never even attempted to paint like that before" – there's this sudden, unexpected lilt to her voice – "they did these beautiful paintings." Brunelle laughs appreciatively, adding that she'd brought some of her own paintings in so that they could get a sense of what she was getting at when she talked about color and composition.

"Y'know," the artist goes on to explain, "abstract work has really a lot of the same elements as any other painting. You have to have a balanced composition: there's use of line and form and color and shape to add interest, there's repetition, there's rhythm. All the basic elements of a good painting are there, whether it be abstract or representational. You just have to have them, or it's not a good painting – it won't be successful." She sees it as being somewhat akin to James Joyce bending the basic elements of literature in a way that wasn't "typical, expected, or linear" in *Finnegan's Wake* or Frank Zappa using his classical training to create his one-of-a-kind so-off-the-beaten-track-we-ain't-never-getting-back-on-it music. "It's the same thing in building a painting as it is in building a story or a piece of music," she maintains. "He [Zappa] had to have that background in order to do what he did."

So, yeah, for Brunelle, it is about that having those elements – that "interesting composition"—in place. But it's also about listening to her intuition instead of having an image set in her mind when she starts out. She tries to clear her mind first, same as she would before meditating. And then she "might choose a color – 'Oh, I really want to use this fluorescent orange today – I really like this color.' And that's kinda where I start. I just want to see what this color looks like, and then I let my hand dictate what I'm going to do with it."

It's a learn-by-going-where-I-have-to-go approach, and her work bears this out. "Effloresence," for instance, is an oil pastel with acrylic: the oil pastel is "like a crayon – a drawing – but then I can go over it and do washes with the acrylic paint[, which] gives it a 'painterly' look." Then there's a collage or what Brunelle calls "a cropped piece," cut down from a much larger one. She picked out the "relevant" elements – some shimmery plastic wrap from a gift basket, a watermelon candy wrapper, and guitar strings that still move instead of being glued in place – from the original, and the result was "Watermelon Song."

"I didn't title it till after it was cropped and done," Brunelle says, "and then I'm like 'Oh!' . . . It wasn't intentionally made to be *that*. It doesn't happen too often where it really comes together." The collage's title, like those of her other works, is just "to get you thinking. Because it's abstract, people don't know what to think." Sometimes, though, "the titles have nothing to do with the work" – she laughs that low musical laugh of hers – "I just like the sound of them."

Nova Scotia Farm Scene

by Tom Morganti

PORTRAIT OF THE ARTIST AS A VET:
TOM MORGANTI

MOST PEOPLE KNOW TOM Morganti as a vet so attuned to the animals he treats, a client once dubbed him "James Herriot." He does everything he can for his patients, even once bringing a young cat with a prolapsed rectum home with him the night before her surgery so that he could monitor her. And he's the only vet I've ever met who writes sympathy notes when one of his patients doesn't make it.

But his work at the Avon Veterinary Clinic in Avon, Connecticut is only part of his story. Morganti is also an artist, painting landscapes, some portraits, and, yes, even an occasional animal study. "I don't have any formal training," he admits, "so everything I learned about painting, I learned trial-and-error." He likes abstract art – has even done some abstract paintings – but sees himself as being "more of an impressionist. I've always been an admirer of Van Gogh . . . in all his phases . . . [and] one of my dreams is to go to Amsterdam and the Van Gogh Museum."

He can't think of a time when he didn't draw, Morganti says. In fact, he still recalls receiving a copy of *The Big*

Book of Animals from his godmother when he was 4 or 5 and trying to draw the animals in the black-and-white photographs. *That,* he maintains, is what got him started and "led to everything else." It's in the blood, though: his mother, Lois Morganti, was a trained artist, and he remembers "her getting a canvas out and me painting alongside her once. And I got so frustrated, I just gave up." His voice is ruefully amused. "I was probably 11 or 12. I can still remember the painting – I wish I still had it, it was the first painting I ever did. It was a still life . . . a pumpkin and something else, like a vase of flowers. It was too much for me: painting was beyond me at that point."

He didn't attempt a painting again until he was at the University of Connecticut. He sold that painting to the dorm's cook for $10, and he hasn't "stopped since." Since then, he has done some commissions and even illustrated a couple of children's books for friends: the books didn't go anywhere, but he takes it all in his philosophical stride. He shows his paintings at the Durham, Connecticut fair every year, and one of his works, "The Black Madonna of Montserrat," was just selected for the New Britain Museum of American Art members' show. He has done shows at McLean's, a convalescent home and assisted-living facility in Simsbury; in fact, the only one-man show that he has done so far was at McLean's. The response was "good," and Morganti sold a couple of paintings. But his own take on this is a little different than you might expect: "Selling them is hard because you know you're never gonna see them again. Give them away, you may not see them, but at least you have a chance, basically. Like children that move away . . . . " He laughs. "It's gone. It's a one-time thing."

Perhaps a good part of that attitude stems from the fact that painting is something that he does mostly for his own satisfaction, "a reflection of your soul." It's not that he isn't tempted to make it a full-time calling, simply that he appreciates how difficult making that happen would be. So he tends to view his art – for the moment, at least – as "a form of therapy . . . a way of de-stressing, of creating something outside of your work place." And yet, as he sees it, there *is* a connection to his work as a vet. "There's an art side of medicine," Morganti reflects. "They're both a combination of left brain and right brain." Not everything is cut and dried, "and when you get results of tests back, you have to look at the patient. So that colors your opinion of where you have to go with a case, but it's really much like art. It unfolds with time . . . especially when your patients can't tell you what's wrong."

Morganti chuckles, then grows more serious as he returns to talking about the creative process. "So you may have an idea in your head what your final product is going to look like, and as you go, it changes. And you see things that work better . . . . It's almost like a birthing process: you don't know what you're going to end up with when you start out."

The conversation periodically comes back Lois Morganti, who died in 2007 of lung cancer. Both his sons, Alex and James, have inherited her artistic ability, he says: Alex, the oldest, has even come up with a kids' book that is "built like a Jacob's ladder – it folds out one way, and then it folds out the other way. It's actually a pretty cool idea." He's encouraging his son start looking for a publisher for it.

He himself has found his own way of bringing his mother into his art. The mural-like landscape that he's currently working on is actually a do-over of a painting of her sons that she was working on towards the end. "She got about a third of the way through and then couldn't do anymore," Morganti recalls. "When she died, one of the things she asked me to do was to use that canvas. She said, 'You either finish it or paint it over." It was, he adds, just too hard for him to try to finish the painting as she'd intended, "so I got some primer and painted it over."

That having been said, Morganti did, he admits, manage to finish a smaller piece of hers . . . well, *almost* the way she would've. He describes it as a "very primitive" painting of five or six men pushing a boat out into the ocean. "I turned the fishermen into saints, and I put Jesus or somebody standing at the stern. And, in the distance, there's a sea monster coming out" – Morganti has trouble controlling his laughter at this point – "of the water with lightning bolts. And I thought, 'Yeah, this is one that Mom would've liked.'"

THE NECK OF A BULL:
KENNY'S BOOKSHOP & ART GALLERIES

F OR MOST OF US, the small bookstore where you could lose yourself in browsing is as rare as Thurber's unicorn in the garden. For Des Kenny, however, this particular unicorn happens to be the family business. Kenny's Bookshop & Art Galleries, Ltd. in Galway, Ireland, has been selling new, used, and out-of-print books since 1940.

"I'm not sure that it's a thing of the past," Kenny says. Granted, in the last 20 years, some small bookstores *have* gone under, he admits: "The world was much colder than they [the owners] expected, and they didn't have the stamina, the knowledge to weather it." But since he started in the business in the mid-'70s, "the number went from four to 20. Only bookstores were selling books then. Now supermarkets, gas stations, discount stores, and Amazon all have encroached on small bookshops." To stay on top it all, "you have to be mad and have a great sense of humor and the neck of a bull."

Kenny's Bookshop has weathered the changes, though, and it has done so by frequently re-inventing

itself. The original store on High Street in the center of
Galway offered, as one writer, Michael Kennedy put it,
"the comfortably cluttered ambience of a home that prized
the importance of written language . . . . Kenny's was
where one might expect to find John Huston perusing an
obscure title when he lived outside Galway in the 1950s,
or John Ford stopping in while filming *The Quiet Man* in
nearby County Mayo, or J. P. Donleavy browsing on leave
from Dublin, as he wrote *The Ginger Man.*"

The art gallery—the first commercially built one
outside of Dublin—came later in 1968. In 1993, Kenny's
went online, becoming the second bookstore in the world
to have its own website. The idea, says Des Kenny, "was to
allow us to develop our online business while maintaining
a retail presence." Thirteen years later, Kenny's moved to
the Liosbaun Retail Estate on Tuam Road in Galway, the
Gallery following in January 2009.

Today, Kennys.ie is Ireland's largest online bookshop,
offering nearly a million titles. They are also getting ready
to "launch a new website which has 6.5 million books
on offer with free postage world-wide and prices that
seriously challenge Amazon as well as other major book
websites," Kenny explains. "The site will also be noted for
the fact that it will maintain the same personal service
that has been our hallmark, continuing our parents'
legacy."

So, that's the shop's past, both distant and not-so-
distant. In the present, Des Kenny admits to "wavering
between pessimism and optimism . . . . I always think
that the worst thing to happen to the book world is the
Harry Potter books. Too much media hype. With all this
push, all this drive, people tend not to make up their own

minds. The whole idea of an individual imagination has not been encouraged, has not been fostered."

E-books? "They're fine in their place [and] will find their place," he says, adding quickly, "It wouldn't be my cup of tea." Then he throws out an observation you don't expect from a bookseller – an entirely accurate observation but an unexpected one, nonetheless. "Books never, never were a major form of entertainment, even in the 19th and early 20th centuries. They would've been for a small percentage [of the population] because they were the most articulate."

That doesn't mean he sees books as being an endangered species. "With every new technology and invention since the radio," he comments, "the amount of books published per annum has increased dramatically. In 1980, 300 books were published—between 2008 and 2009, 2,000 books were published. There has been at least a five – to ten-fold growth in Ireland, a small country." And while these figures are "specific to Ireland," he imagines that "it is much the same world-wide, probably even more so in countries where literacy has experienced a dramatic growth."

And there's still a solid interest in rare and out-of-print books, which the shop deals in . . . books that "wouldn't be on the front desk, but they are accessible to the public." Book lovers come for them "in waves. Sometimes we have loads, and sometimes we have none . . . . [For] the person who likes the feel of the book, the way it smells, it's a tactile thing that can't be replicated for now, at least. There are still things you can't get on the Web."

It's a business that Kenny loves everything about. "When I open the door in the morning with the key, I never know what to expect," he says. "It's a constant flow of customers, new books, and interesting people. A bookshop is the most democratic of stores. It is both the genesis and the flowering of books, it is a place where ideas and imagination are welcome, it is the Mecca of the Imagination."

Related links:

- http://kennys.ie

Always a Gift: Wendy Van Welie
& Indigo Images

PHOTOGRAPHER WENDY VAN WELIE isn't exactly Dr. Doolittle. She has, however, had encounters with wild animals that the good doctor himself might've envied. And listening to her talk about her photographic safaris, you realize that it's really not about being able to speak to the animals – it's about the animals being able to speak to us in their own "words" and their own way. About our being sensitive enough to listen.

Which Van Welie is. Right now, she's telling me the story behind the large cheetah photograph hanging in her Indigo Images Photography Studio & Gallery in Granby, Connecticut. In that photo, a mother cheetah relaxes with her cubs, her amber eyes thoughtful, utterly serene . . . a Madonna in a spotted fur suit. "She was that calm," the photographer remembers. "She was watchful, though: she was keeping an eye on the babies, she wasn't moving, she was making sure they were close at hand. But very gentle, very peaceful. She allowed us in. She could have easily taken them and moved off. But she allowed us to just sit with her while she was feeding them."

The safaris started for Van Welie when she was young – "My dad took us on safari every year. You know, living in South Africa, it was easy" – but she didn't actually take photography courses until she came to this country years later. "My kids were little, and I struggled with that," she explains. "I was always a better mom working than not. I *needed* to build an identity of my own. What I was given was a special skill that made it possible to go back to school." She enrolled at Hennepin Technical College in Minnesota, earning an associates degree in commercial photography while doing work in fashion photography and photojournalism as well.

Flash forward to the present, and you find Van Welie doing many of the gigs you'd expect any commercial photographer to be doing: weddings, graduation photos, and family portraits. But she brings her photojournalistic training to bear on them, drawing out the story or expression that other eyes might have missed. "I love, love, love working with people," she says. "I have an absolute passion for the craft."

She's a traditionalist when it comes to that craft, loving the smell of chemicals and "darkroom stuff." And while Van Welie appreciates that digital photography enables us to "get those shots we never could've anticipated in the past," she also believes that it makes it "too easy for us to shoot quickly and not anticipate and wait." She has some concerns about Photoshop as well: "I struggled ethically with that because I just feel that it's no longer the craft and the art of giving that beautiful shot . . . . those moments that no amount of Photoshop could change. You could extract it – you could do a lot to it – but it's about catching that moment in space. As soon as you start changing it, it's no longer that moment."

Catching the moment . . . that phrase and variations on it show up a lot in Van Welie's conversation. She's acutely aware of it, especially when she's on photographic safari with her husband Gordon. As she sees it, "the charm of any experience is the joy of *not* being able to do it again – [of] knowing that that encounter, no matter how long or how fleeting, is gone, you will never get it again. You may get a different one – you may encounter a different lion, you may encounter a different cheetah, you may encounter a different elephant – but that moment is gone forever, never to be recreated." The animals are un-posable and inevitably dictate the situation. "They're going to tell you when they want the camera in and when they don't. And it's learning how to step back, give them two minutes, step back in, and get the camera comfortable between you and them." Otherwise, she cautions, you can kill the moment *and* the animals' trust.

Then, too, there's the matter of having the right equipment and really knowing the animal you're working with. Otters, for instance, "move quickly – elephants don't. So, when I'm shooting elephants, I can miss a couple and be patient. You move very slowly with cheetahs. When I'm shooting flying cheetahs, I can't shoot on schedule. It's very different."

Ask Van Welie to name one safari experience that stands out above all the rest in her mind, and she won't. "When you go on safari," she insists, "every session is a treasure, an absolute treasure. So I don't know if I can choose one. Obviously my cheetahs – I just loved, loved the mom and her babies, that was such a perfect environment to just sit and visit . . . . The lions are fantastic to shoot because they're so lovable. They lick your hand. They're not as anxious or as high-strung as the cheetah. They linger, so you can get a long session with a lion and be very satisfied with what you get . . . . The zebras are beautiful. I have a passion for the zebra, hence my zebra logo." Even the elephants, whom she feels "a little wary" around, are fascinating to her.

"We came across a herd of elephants once," she recalls. "Elephants herd as females, and they bring the little ones in the middle. So, as they move, they have this *nursery* of babies that are protected by their mums and the grandmums. We got a bit close, and one of the grammies, she came right up to the Land Rover. She was waving her ears, and she was just . . . she was *angry*: 'Do not come any closer because these are our babies. Yeah, these are *our* babies.' And they let us stay. We could shoot, but we had to stay far."

Moments like these – the times that the lions, the cheetahs, and the elephants allow her into their world – are "always a gift," says Van Welie. Perhaps she might view it differently were she shooting them in a zoo where "there isn't a place for them to escape to." But photographing these animals in the wild as she does, she really does see it all as "a treasure hunt – it's finding them and knowing that you'll be able to walk away satisfied, even if it was just a glimpse."

She sometimes thinks of putting together a book of wildlife photos. "It's ultimately the time involved of just giving the treasure," Van Welie reflects. "In fact, if I had to choose here and now, I would *love* to do a book on flowers. I love color, and flowers give that to me. And, again, it's a little bit like shooting wildlife: every picture is different." The challenge is trying to capture the way we see a rose, for instance, in our minds, "the *feeling* of the flower . . . the essence, the symmetry, and the perfection you get. There is such a wonder in shooting, whether it's wild animals or wildflowers. And it's that fleeting moment that is, for me, the treasure." Her voice becomes more matter-of-fact as she returns to this particular moment. "Yes, I would love to do a book. But I think that the first one would have to be on the flowers."

Related links:

- www.indigoimagesllc.com.

Wendy Birchall

Soul Readings: Wendy Birchall & Earth Angel Design

WENDY BIRCHALL'S NOT WHAT immediately comes to mind when you think of someone who does readings. She has an M. A. in exercise physiology and ran corporate fitness centers for years; taught courses at Westfield State College; made soap and Christmas wreaths; worked as a floral designer and a Wilton cake decorator; and has raised three children while doing all this. Come to think of it, she could easily be mistaken for a typical suburban wife and mom.

But once you start talking to Birchall, you realize how wrong that picture is. The owner and driving force behind Earth Angel Design in Southwick, Massachusetts, she is an earnest, articulate personality . . . very much her own woman, well at ease . . . and all of that comes across in her conversation. Especially when she's talking about all things spiritual.

"I was born and raised Catholic," Birchall says. That upbringing gave her "a great base," but there were "things that didn't feel right – things that I disagreed with on a spiritual level, not even so much a conscious level. Like living one time—trying to get it right in one lifetime. To me, it couldn't be done in one lifetime. And just some other ideas that I didn't agree with."

She had always been drawn to mediums and psychics. "But I always felt that I was doing something wrong by doing that," Birchall says, laughing a little ruefully. "So there was that fear part of me that kept me from pursuing it."

She got there eventually and inadvertently, however. A friend who had just lost her sister consulted a medium: the medium "brought her sister through in conversation, and it was such a profound experience. I saw the healing that happened with my friend and said aloud for the first time, 'I really wish I had the ability to do something like that.'" Birchall's friend looked at her and said, "Wendy, go pick up a book. You know, there's books on this stuff." And, in time, she happened upon the right book – *Open to Channel,* which focused on "finding a connection with your spirit guides. They never really mentioned angels . . . just finding that connection with your higher self. And, as I read it, things started to happen – to change – and I realized that as long as my intention was good and that I knew where I wanted to be with it, I could do that. And that's what began this whole journey."

Freed from her old fear, she visited a medium. The latter told Birchall that she could best open up her latent female energy or *kundalini* ("Which, to me at the time, sounded like a pasta product – I had to ask her what it was," Birchall laughs.) by learning Reiki. It seemed like a good enough place to begin. She took to the Japanese form of energy healing quickly, finding in it "that feeling of a connection to something greater than you that is so meaningful and so beautiful." That Reiki experience found its way into her book *A Sojourn with the Soul*, the story of her spiritual awakening. She learned to trust what she felt – to let herself be guided by the energy feedback she was getting from the people she worked with. "I used Reiki specifically with my dad a year-and-a-half ago when he passed away," she explains. "But I used it more as a way of helping him make that transition – not asking for anything but allowing the energy to bring him comfort and peace as he was in the process of crossing over."

Like most spiritual journeys, there was a certain amount of meandering involved. But she did have a guide—the Archangel Aaron, who came to her during an early guided meditation.

"I didn't know that it was an angel at first," she admits. "He didn't have any wings: he was just this beautiful man . . . . He never told me that he was an angel. But I'd get into my car, and there'd be an angel song on." One song in particular seemed to come on whenever she did her meditations: "It wasn't a popular song, but it was always on. So he was giving me hints, but I wasn't quite picking up on them." Only when she was spiritually ready, she adds, did she realize that an angel was trying to make contact – *her* guardian angel.

Under Aaron's guidance, Birchall began keeping the journal that was the basis for *Sojourn*. At the time, she didn't view herself as much of a writer or a reader: journaling, however, helped her to see "the synchronicities, how things were coming into my life. And many of the experiences were so profound that had I not written them down immediately, I would've doubted the fact that they had happened."

Earth Angel Design was another offshoot of her journey. At present, the business' main emphasis is jewelry: the stones used are aligned with the various archangels that Birchall draws her inspiration from. She also carries angel essences and has a high-school girl who "is drawing me some angel portraits. They're beautiful, and I hope I can reproduce them [so that] people can purchase them." Then, too, there's an angel box coming out, "kinda like a God box where you can put your thoughts. Or you can put a special stone in it or angel jewelry – whatever feels right."

And then there are the readings.

Twice a week, Birchall does her readings, using a deck of angel cards. She herself is clairaudient, so the cards are really visuals for her clients: "I could have a conversation with you, and the angels would just kind of bring themselves through." The cards simply help drive the messages home. She doesn't deal in predictions, she adds; her messages are always rooted "in the here and now. You have to live in the moment. That's the greatest message." She speaks, if possible, even more earnestly. "So it's more a guiding versus a telling, and people are more open to it."

Along those lines, she views herself as a kind of teacher trying to "give them the skills and spark their interest enough that when they leave here, they can start on their own journey." Birchall doesn't encourage her clients to come back. She takes very seriously the warning about consulting soothsayers in the Old Testament. "I think it's there to really protect. What is our purpose when we come down here? It's our job to figure out what it is. If you're handing it over for someone else to do, you haven't met your goal here on earth."

So, that's about where Birchall is right now – doing readings, sending out queries about her book, and becoming increasingly involved in every aspect of her business. It's all another leg of her journey, she says, and it suits her. Before Earth Angel Design, she "was Wendy the Wanderer," Birchall laughs. "That's what my name means, and I felt like I was living up to it. I always hated that, but now I'm embracing it." She has her "fingers in so many different things, there's no possible way I'm going to be bored . . . . You have to follow your passion. That's really what it comes down to, and everything else will happen."

Related link:

■ http://www.earthangeldesign.com

Anna Bresnerkoff Cohen

A Working Life: Anna Bresnerkoff Cohen

*In honor of Women's History Month, I am re-running an interview that first appeared in **Hartford Woman** back in May 1987. The subject: my Great-Aunt Anna Bresnerkoff Cohen (1902 – 2001), a hard-working well-read to-the-point woman with a heart and spirit as big as she was short (very) and a truly impressive stage whisper. We need to celebrate the Anna Cohens, those not-so-commonplace women in our family trees. They just don't make 'em like that anymore.*

****

S HE HAS CUT DOWN her volunteer work at the Outpatient Pediatric Clinic at Hartford Hospital to two mornings a week instead of three, but that's the only concession that my great-aunt has made to being 87.

"I love the work I'm doing," says Anna Cohen, who leaves her apartment in West Hartford, Connecticut punctually every Monday and Tuesday morning to punch, sort, file, and collate the slips about the clinic's patients. "The only thing is, when I don't finish something, it's still there when I come back next week." Once in awhile, she considers giving up the work: "But I gotta have something else in mind before I do it."

Cohen is no stranger to work. She came over from Russia as a small child in the early 1900s; as soon as she and her sister Mary were old enough, they went to work at the now-defunct G. Fox department store in downtown Hartford during the summers.

"We made the big pay of three-and-a-half dollars," Cohen recalls. "We gave my mother the envelope, she gave us 50 cents, and we thought we were millionaires, both Mary and I." Every cent counted, so everybody who could work did: even Cohen's mother, busy raising both her own children and her stepchildren, peddled notions door-to-door in the adjoining tenement houses.

"My mother could not speak English, and the people she approached usually wouldn't let her in. She showed them the basket, and they picked out what they wanted. She eventually learned to talk English, very broken, but she was understood, and she understood the people."

Cohen worked in several stores until shortly after her marriage to my grandmother's youngest brother, Iz. "From then on, I was a housewife," she says. "I didn't have to go to work. Iz never wanted me to go to work, and it was unheard of that a woman would go to work, especially if you had children. We didn't have nurseries like they do now where we could put our children; and if there were any, which I didn't have knowledge of, it was rather expensive."

So she stayed at home until 1942. Then her oldest son, Sidney, went into the service and her daughter, Ruthie, left for college, leaving only her 9-year-old son Jerry. She got a part-time job in the fabrics department at Sage-Allen, and her mother looked after Jerry in the afternoons when he got home from school. Iz, suffering from heart disease, was too ill to work himself or raise any objections to her doing so.

"During the time that I worked," Cohen explains, "he was at home, more or less taking care of himself. And, to be honest with you, I never knew when I came home whether I'd find a corpse or a man. He shouldn't have been left alone, but we were in dire straits. There was no income coming in, and what little I was earning – which was, part-time, $26 a week – was a gold mine to me. At least it covered the table."

Cohen worked at Sage's until after World War II, when the part-timers were laid off, "and things were quieter. During the war, people bought like crazy, whether they needed it or not." Iz died in 1948; she remained at home a year and then, not wanting to be dependent on anybody, went to work at Aetna Life and Casualty. Her life from then on until she retired at 65 in 1966, became "a working life."

Even after retirement, however, Cohen still worked. She tried her hand at babysitting at the Y in West Hartford. Around the same time, she also started volunteering at Hartford Hospital, working in a number of departments there before she found her present job at the Outpatient Pediatric Clinic.

"And that's what I do now," she says simply. "They're very pleased with me; but, by the same token, I'm pleased, too, because it's a lot for me as well as for them . . . . I found my niche here, and I like it. They've been very wonderful to me. And, in spite of the fact that I don't get any money, I enjoy it tremendously, and I look forward to it."

Making a Difference:
Dr. Andrew J. Ponichtera

" **Y**OU KNOW, IT'S REALLY kind of in between everything," says Dr. Andrew J. Ponichtera. He's sitting in his dental office in Weatogue, Connecticut, explaining his specialty, maxillofacial rehabilitation. "It's a little bit being an artist – it's a little bit being a dentist – it's a little bit being a sculptor – it's a little bit of everything. It's a little bit playing with models." He laughs gently at himself, then grows serious. "But the thing is, you really do get to provide a service a service that really is very satisfactory – satisfactory for both you and the patient."

More than satisfactory, really. For people with some type of facial impairment – a cleft palate, a missing ear or nose – maxillofacial rehabilitation means the difference between feeling comfortable about going out in public and not. It's that simple. And that crucial.

Ponichtera came to the field by a fairly straightforward route. He'd always been "a little bit mechanically inclined and liked to play with models and stuff like that." In college, he hung out with two of his cousins: a dentist and a medical student who eventually became a pulmonologist. He quickly realized that he wasn't cut out for pulmonology. Seeing "people that are really, really sick" bothered him, he admitted. He "couldn't tolerate that emotionally. I just would go home and feel like crying." Dentistry, on the other hand, "was nice – you got to do a lot of interesting things." Plus, it appealed to that mechanical side of his nature—his inner engineer, if you will. "So it became a natural extension, and I decided to go ahead and do that."

He graduated from dental school in 1977 and started his residency at Sinai Hospital in Detroit. There he met his first maxillofacial prosthetist, a man who was doing "all the interesting things that I really liked to do." The prosthetist let the young resident spend time with him while he worked with kids with cleft palates or with cancer patients who were missing eyes, ears, noses, or parts of jaws. And Ponichtera, who'd found pulmonology so difficult to handle, had no trouble dealing with people who were disfigured in some way. Here, at least, he could do something, and he "thought that was really cool." But he wasn't 100% sure at that point and ended up going into dentistry instead.

After a couple of years "doing mundane dentistry—doing fillings and seeing lots of people," however, Ponichtera was ready to try something different. He got into a three-year program at the Mayo Clinic, one of the few facilities that offered residencies in maxillofacial prosthetics then. "We spent lots of time with plastic surgeons [and with] ear-nose-and-throat guys," he recalls. "We spent almost six months being residents with those guys. It was interesting, rewarding . . . a specialty where patients really need your help. So it goes from seeing kids with cleft palates and speech problems to kids with craniofacial dystosis [morphic facial growth, Elephant Man's Disease being one form] that are missing ears, cancer patients, and trauma patients."

Ponichtera eventually made his way to the University of Connecticut Health Center in Farmington, where he worked for awhile as part of the craniofacial team for kids. Now, working out of his Weatogue office, he does more with "patients that are either missing ears or parts of their face and adults with cancer." But he doesn't do it surgically – he does it "with plastic and so-called 'pieces.'" For the college student who "loved working with putty and being a sculptor, it's a natural transition. I really like it. It's a lot of fun."

There's more to it than that, naturally. Compassion is key, and Ponichtera has plenty to spare. You need, he says, "a certain mentality to see people—some of whom are grossly disfigured, some of whom really smell" because of necrotic tissue. So it's a matter of seeing beyond all that? I ask. "You have to *do* beyond all that," he counters quietly. "Your staff has to be attentive to that. You can't yell, 'Oh, God!' You just have to accept them as being normal, and everybody here is good at that." The staff gets involved in other ways, too: "We've made some really interesting prostheses, and they end up stitching head bands together to help hold on a facial prosthesis."

He touches briefly on Frances Derwent Wood, the British sculptor who devised electroplated masks for disfigured soldiers during World War I. This was where maxillofacial prosthetics really started, Ponichtera insists

– with Wood and others trying to help men "that wouldn't have survived before. A lot of traumatic injuries, different weapons . . . . It really came by default into the hands of dentistry." Now the field is "an acknowledged specialty or sub-specialty of dentistry that's been around quite awhile. But the bulk of it came in World War I and World War II – a lot of changes, a lot of new techniques."

Of course, with implants and more sophisticated technology, that picture is changing once more. There's even talk about doing much of the work via CAD/CAM software. And now, Ponichtera explains, "almost all of the oral surgeons, almost all of the programs are gonna be M. D. programs. They have much more training in facial and plastic surgery, and they're getting out of the role of just taking out teeth. But there's still a select population that can't be treated surgically. And that's where I come in."

A lot of kids missing ears get sent over from Connecticut Children's Medical Center (CCMC) in Hartford, for instance. He'll make a diagnostic wax-up or guide for where the implants need to be; later, after Dr. Richard Bevilaequa at CCMC has surgically placed the screw, Ponichtera will "attach a silicone ear to it. Clips in – clips off. We've done noses that way – clip in and clip off – and, well, you don't have to worry about it. It stays on." In the past, they would've had to glue the prostheses on.

Sometimes his creativity really gets a work-out, Ponichtera admits. They've had a couple of people come in "who have been missing almost half their face, and you really can't put implants in because" – there's a long, thoughtful but matter-of-fact pause – "they're kinda at the end stage of life. But you can make them a prosthesis, and they become a little more socially acceptable. And that's kinda cool."

He shows me a model. "The ear is over here," he says. "We make it out of wax so that we can basically boil it out." That leaves him with a model to put the silicone in; the silicone then cures with a little bit of heat. He brings out more forms: one for a patient without an eye, another for a cancer patient missing part of a jaw. (The latter has an obturator for closing the opening of the palate.) He keeps the individual molds in case the patients ever need replacements parts. "I mean, I could make another ear for this patient without his being here. And I have a record of what colors they use . . . . We used to mix up all our own colors." He laughs. "Like art class. Now they have kits that are available. But I still have my own colors that I like to use. Just gets you a *little* bit better customization."

In fact, Ponichtera really prefers doing the whole process himself. He gets a stronger sense of what works for the patient that way. And he's not above bringing his work home with him. "My wife gets a little bit upset with me at times because" – he chuckles – "I'll be doing this in the basement for a few hours."

So, what would Derwent Wood say to it all? "He'd be amazed at how much it had changed," Ponichtera concedes. "But the principles haven't changed." He himself appreciates the technological advancements but still leans toward the hand-crafted. "And that's what I get out of it," he says. "It's like you put your little heart and soul in the whole thing, and it's yours. And I think there's more value in it than if it's just done by computer or manufactured."

Maggie's Gift: Barb Borkowski & The Healing Journey

THERE IS, BARB BORKOWSKI says, an old photo of her resting her hand atop the head of her great-grandfather's collie. "I was two-years-old," the animal communicator recalls. "I sensed that his head hurt." Right from the beginning, she was an empath where animals were concerned: "I grew up with several beagles that my dad used for hunting. Spending time with them was my preferred activity. If one of them did not feel well, I felt the discomfort in my body."

Borkowski, a licensed massage therapist, energy therapist, and Reiki practitioner, owns The Healing Journey in Steubenville, Ohio. "All living things are composed of energy," she writes on her website. "The life force flows through the body. Stress, illness and emotional conflicts may cause a disturbance in the flow. Energy Therapy assists the body in returning to a balanced state." Animals aren't her only clients, however. She also works with people – autistic children, for instance, and adults who are in comas or unable to speak as a result of stroke damage. Reading people, like

reading animals, has always come easily to her. When
she was a nurse, she "was able to guess what physical
problems newly admitted patients had just by looking
at them. A few co-workers knew about my ability. Test
results always confirmed my initial assessment of the
health problems."

It was a long time before she fully understood this ability
of hers, though. A car accident changed all that. Trying
to ease the pain, Borkowski began going for massage
therapy: and she became interested enough to enroll in
massage therapy classes herself. There she learned not
only "about the energy fields of all living things" but that
"there was finally a name" for what she did.

Borkowski's work with people "incorporate[s] subtle
healing energy with massage techniques. The combination
allows the positive flow to enter the body and supports
the release of negativity from stress. The result is total
relaxation." So, yes, she does have human clients who
come to her for energy therapy on a regular basis. But
she's mostly in demand as an animal communicator.
"People tend to seek help for their pets before they will for
themselves," she explains. "The main service I provide for
animals is communication. When I make on-site calls,
I use Reiki while relaying the information to the owners
about their pet. When working remotely, I look at a picture
of the animal." Simply by studying the photo, she can tell
what's bothering the cat, dog, or horse: the info "comes
into my mind, and I write it down. The majority of issues
are related to the home environment. Animals are very
sensitive to human emotions." So, distance healing or
communication "involves the pet owners, not just the
pets."

Sometimes she finds that the problem is inadequate nutrition; other times, there's an underlying health issue. Once, when Borkowski touched a horse, she "immediately felt like I had a stomach ulcer." A gastroscopy performed a few days later showed that the horse had definite ulceration: she was put on medication and improved rapidly. Another horse wasn't so lucky. During a phone session, Borkowski sensed that he had stomach cancer, but the owner didn't look into getting tests done. The horse died a few months later. The autopsy showed that Borkowski's reading had been all too true.

Most of the people who go to the trouble of consulting an animal communicator do follow through on what she tells them, however. And the animals themselves "desire to be healthy. They are open to healing. When helping them in person, I receive many 'kisses' from dogs once their thoughts are told."

Empaths generally pay a price for their gift, and Borkowski is no exception. Once, she volunteered at a local shelter, and she "could feel all of the anxiety, loneliness, fear, and desire to be out of the cages." The animals' excitement at seeing "people arrive with the hope that someone would take them out of the shelter and the sad eyes watching them leave hurt so much. I cried every time I went there."

"When you are hopelessly lost," British novelist Elizabeth Goudge wrote, "follow your animals." To Borkowski, who shares Goudge's passion for dogs, those words suggest "that people should strive to be more like their pets. The qualities of being non-judgmental, loyal, and givers of unconditional love are admirable traits of our four-legged friends."

You see, for her, dogs have been more than tried-and-true friends: they have also been teachers who have helped her grow as both a healer and a person. "As an adult, I picked sick pups," Borkowski reflects. "I did not know at the time they were ill, but I was able to assist with their healing." So she learned from them in that sense. Her most important teacher, however, was a determined yellow Labrador retriever, Maggie. "I had the privilege of sharing almost 12 years with her. When Maggie wanted something, she stood still and stared until someone noticed. One day, she had a prolonged stare. I tried to figure out what she wanted. She stomped her front paws on the dining-room floor, and these words came to mind: 'You are supposed to help God's gentle creatures.' That was the day I decided to include animal communication as part of my business. Thank you, Maggie . . . . What a journey it has been."

Related link:

■ http://www.thehealingjourneync.wordpress.com

The Queen's Scribe: Claire Ridgway & The Anne Boleyn Files

SHE WAS STANDING IN a crowd, Claire Ridgway remembers, her eyes fixed on the elegantly dressed black-haired woman standing on the scaffold. It was May 19, 1536, and the woman was Anne Boleyn, condemned to death on trumped-up charges of adultery and incest. As she listened to the queen's final speech, Ridgway was "completely overcome with horror that this innocent woman was going to be executed . . . . Even now, I can remember being rooted to the spot and being so terrified that I could not speak. I just couldn't believe that this brutal act was really going to happen before my eyes and that nobody was going to stop it."

Fortunately, Ridgway woke up before the final bit of swordplay by the French executioner that Anne's husband, Henry VIII, had specially sent for. (Men really don't know how to give gifts like they used to.) The nightmare left her in a cold sweat . . . and with a most unusual epiphany. She shook her husband, Tim, awake and told him that she was going to start a website called The Anne Boleyn Files "to educate people about Anne's real story."

And she did. The Anne Boleyn Files (TABF) started in February 2009, designed by her husband—a man who nowadays matter-of-factly refers to himself as an "Anne Boleyn widower." She "had no idea that anybody would ever find the site," says the British-born writer, who lives with her family near the Alhambra in Spain. "So it started out just as a diary of my research into Anne's life, my journey to the truth, and it still is today." That journey has had an amazing impact on her life: she no longer freelances, and she spends much of her day researching the Tudor period and writing about Henry's second wife. "I've grown so much as a person," she remarks, "and love the fact that I'm finally doing a job that I love and that I have a real purpose in my life. There's nothing better than writing an article on Anne and then reading comments from people who really learned something from my work – that is so fulfilling!"

Historian Eric Ives (*The Life and Death of Anne Boleyn*) has himself called Anne "the third woman in my life after my immediate family," adding that it "is true once she interests you, fascination grows, as it did for men at the time, and finally for Henry himself." Ridgway and I discuss this fascination, which has led to so many books (fiction and non-fiction) and dramatizations about Anne. Why, more than 475 years after her execution, does it still endure? "I think it's a combination of the tragedy of her story, the awful miscarriage of justice she suffered, the love story between her and Henry VIII, . . . and the myths that surround her," the writer reflects.

Indeed, it's a story that has "all the ingredients of a good romance and even a thriller." Like Ives, she believes that somehow the luckless queen's "magnetic personality reaches through the ages and grabs us." The novel that best captures this for Ridgway is Jean Plaidy's *Murder Most Royal* (1949), which "really brings Anne to life without maligning her in any way." And her favorite Anne movie is "Anne of the Thousand Days." She especially loves "the scene where Henry visits Anne in the Tower, and Genevieve Bujold, as Anne, gives that amazing speech about how it will be her daughter who will be queen and that her blood will have been well spent. I so wish Anne had really had the chance to give that speech!"

Aside from TABF, Ridgway has also written a resource guide to all things Anne Boleyn – newspaper/magazine articles; details about places that figure into her story; podcasts; fact sheets; portraits, heraldry, and crests; archives and documents; poetry, stories, and music; movies and videos; and much more. ((For more information on that guide, check the website.) And somewhere further down the line, Ridgway would like to write a non-fiction account of Anne's life.

But it doesn't stop there. She has also created a sister site, The Elizabeth Files, which is – you got it – about Elizabeth I, Anne's greatest legacy to England. The writer sees the Virgin Queen as being "her mother's daughter in so many ways. Both Henry and Anne were highly intelligent people, so Elizabeth inherited that from both of them; but she definitely had her mother's magnetism, wit, charm, perseverance, passion, and hot temper. She also had Anne's 'way with men.' Don't get me wrong – I don't believe that either woman was a 'tart' or an outrageous flirt, but Elizabeth knew how to 'work' the men she was surrounded by. She was a woman in a man's world, but she managed to gain the undying loyalty and love of the men advising her. She inherited that skill from her mother."

You're bound to take a few hits when you're in love, and Ridgway has taken them – on the home front, no less: "Researching her [Anne] every working day has obviously made her and her family a huge part of my life and has had a knock-on effect with my family." She ruefully tells me about the day her kids were making gingerbread men: her youngest boy bit the head off his and exclaimed, "Ooooh, look, Mum, it's Anne Boleyn!" She is, she admits, "very fond of the whole Boleyn family and get very annoyed when they are maligned."

Indeed, you can tell from both the tone of the blog and her comments that Anne has become an old friend to her – someone whom she knows almost as well she does herself. That being the case, what sort of woman does she feel Henry's second queen would've become had she been allowed to live out her life? "I think if Anne had been given a chance, she would have eventually had a son," Ridgway reflects, "and this would have cemented hers and Henry's marriage. She was a patron of the arts, had an interest in charity, education, and architecture, and so I believe that she would have continued being a good queen and a worthy consort and partner to Henry."

Related links:

— http://www.theanneboleynfiles.com
— http://www.elizabethfiles.com

A LASTING RESONANCE: DEANE G. KELLER

(Another from The Way-Back Files – An interview with artist and sculptor Deane G. Keller, February 1982.)

****

"Drawing offers a unique record of an encounter with a culture of experience transformed from fleeting moment to lasting resonance."

—Deane G. Keller (1940 – 2005)

****

L IKE A CHARACTER FROM one of Thomas Hardy's novels, the figure about to head out over the wind-stirred field seems dwarfed by the vast sky and landscape. Yet that figure in its rough hat and jacket doesn't strike us as being insignificant somehow. Pausing on the edge of the field, squarely confronting the horizon, it has a certain defiance about it – almost as though it's striking out against a painfully beautiful, indifferent and unexpected universe. The great horizontals in the painting are, in its creator Deane G. Keller's words, "broken, brought into focus by one little vertical figure."

The image is one that repeats itself in Hardy's novels, which are a passion of Keller's. "The sense of scale is evident in his work," the Marlborough, Connecticut-based artist explains, "and to the painter also. The idea under the surface in all Hardy's work is that man acts out his destiny, defines himself against an expanded landscape."

Keller, a painter and sculptor whose work has received numerous awards (among them, the Copley Winter Exhibition First prize in 1969), teaches painting, life drawing, anatomy, and art history at the Lyme Academy of Fine Arts in Old Lyme. He and other members of the faculty there are intent on reviving the tradition of Connecticut Impressionism. Since June, the majority of the classes have been taught in the new Foundation of the Arts Building: that building sits where the Connecticut Impressionists did much of their work at the turn of the century. Last fall, a film crew shot some scenes near the academy as well as in and around the town itself for a film on American Impressionism being produced by the Smithsonian Institute.

The artists' colony established there by Florence Griswold in 1885 was one of the earliest in America. They were influenced by the current trends in French painting at the time: rural subjects painted in outdoor settings, unfinished painting surfaces, and "a romantic delight in color." Among the first artists working out of the Old Lyme colony were Will Howe Foote and Lewis Cohen, who, working in the Barbizon style, emphasized rich but muted colors and man's bond with nature. Later, with the arrival of Childs Hassam and Walter Griffin in 1903, many of the painters began experimenting with French Impressionist techniques – short, bright abstract brushwork and flat composition. The revival of this tradition, says Keller, signified "a return to nature as a source of art."

And that is part of where his sense of connection with Hardy comes in. He has been fascinated with the British novelist's work since high school – not just with Hardy's characters but also with his emphasis on man's mysterious relationship with nature. Keller's love for the novels has kept pace with his development as an artist. Rambling along the southern coast of England during his last visit . . . visiting the Roman ruins there (both he and his wife Dorothy, an Assistant Professor of Fine Arts at St. Joseph College in West Hartford, share a deep interest in archaeology) . . . enjoying "the sense of history underfoot," he talks now about picking up the author's trail and exploring the places which "he [Hardy] knew and could describe so well."

Keller moves over to another painting, one of a green field merging with a yellow wheat-filled one, the sky a rich subtle blend of grays and purples with duller touches of rose. "Supposedly, Gabriel Oak in *Far from the Madding Crowd* lived here," he says. It's almost as though he's talking about an old friend. "And over here" – the artist gestures beyond the fields to a point not encompassed by the canvas – "Bathsheba Everdene lived.

"I drove into this driveway," Keller continues with a faint smile, "and asked, 'Pardon me for intruding, but is this where Bathsheba Everdene lived?' The woman, who was very pleasant and responsive, said, 'Absolutely. And this is the bay window where she stood and looked out at Oak's hut.'"

What Keller has done is to translate the images from Hardy's books into a visual media. The novelist was an artist of sorts himself: like his character Jude in *Jude the Obscure*, he had been trained as an architect and produced a number of sketches during his lifetime. Perhaps, Keller reflects, this explains why his writing has that intensely visual quality—and why those "one-shot" images of startling vividness and clarity can make the leap from printed page to canvas so well.

"There was a constant resonance with his own experience and past which kept his work so animated and life-like," Keller says. "As a painter, I have to deal with form and color. But my painter's goal is to go beyond the form to the idea. Maybe his way of looking at things has become a vehicle for me – has become a vantage point. Some of his quality of looking at the world is readily adaptable for me as a painter."

Hardy had a strong feeling for nature's beauty and aloofness, something that Keller subtly plays upon in his paintings. It's definitely a soul-met-soul connection: his empathy for the writer comes across both in his art and his conversation. Looking at a third painting – that of a road in Higher Bockhampton that Hardy walked as a youngster – Keller muses, "I daresay it was on this walk, a solitary sort of walk, that he picked up his feeling for nature.

"Hardy was sensitive to all sides – not just to writing – but there are probably images which we will never know. His own private responses to nature, some of which we know from the novels. Some may have taken the form of drawings, like the sketches he did in Cornwall."

He talks about doing a portrait of Hardy himself and shows me a small preliminary study in oils. The writer's craggy set face looks out at us with a reflective, somewhat bitter expression, eyebrows permanently arched in wry amusement. In it, we see the man who, "crushed" by the public outcry against his novels, turned to writing poetry. Who viewed life with all its ironies as a general drama of pain, only occasionally lightened with flickerings of happiness.

"He has a broad, broad speculative look," Keller observes quietly from where he stands. "I would like to have two qualities developed [in the painting]. One is the facticity of the fellow. The other aspect is how very remote, distant he could be as his mind took him through sketches from his own past."

Sally Logue

Soul-Catcher: Sally Logue

Inlaid and incised soul-catchers were the most important items used by curing shamans. When sickness was believed to be the result of the soul leaving the body, a shaman could be hired to search for the errant soul which he enticed to enter the soul-catcher. With the apertures at either end securely plugged with cedar bark stoppers, the soul could be safely carried back to the patient and restored.

—*Norman Bancroft-Hunt*

****

SHE LIKES TO START on the eyes as soon as possible in her portraits, artist Sally Logue explains. "It's important to get them right. I usually start with a rough outline of the head and then work from the eyes outwards. You'd be taught to work from top left to bottom, gradually building up color and tone, but I like the eyes to bring the portrait to life early on." They really are "the windows to the soul," she says, and they speak to her.

They speak to the viewer, too. The animals and birds in Logue's portraits draw us in with their eyes. A wistful Blue-cream Point Siamese . . . an elfin Ruddy Abyssinian . . . an inquisitive Springer spaniel . . . two British Giant rabbits looking like they're chatting companionably over a lettuce lunch . . . all of them are vivid presences, seemingly ready to step off the pastel paper and become fully dimensional. Logue has a strong rapport with her subjects, and it shows in every pastel-penciled line. The word that keeps coming up in her customers' comments is "captured," and they're not always talking about a physical likeness. More often than not, their remarks have to do with intangibles: "you captured their spirit," "you've managed to capture so much about them . . . it really does look as if you know Simon and Barney well," or "her character is captured totally." Some folks even admit to crying upon receiving a portrait of a deceased pet. "I don't feel like I'm looking at a portrait and it really brings it home that he is no longer with us," one customer wrote.

"Someone did a 'Wordle' of my customer comments," recalls the artist, who works out of her home in Cumbria, England, "and you're right – the words 'captured' and 'likeness' and 'absolutely' came up top of the list, my customers are so kind!"

Her first portraits were for local clients: they'd bring their pets to her, and she'd take photos to work from. "This gave me a chance to study the animals closely and pick out individual characteristics," she observes. "If you have three similar black Labs running round your feet, you may think they all look the same; but studying and comparing their photos make it much easier to tell them apart." Now that she receives commissions from other countries, she often exchanges "several e-mails with the client to discuss their photos and help choose one to work from which brings out that spark of personality."

Over the years, Logue's artwork has made some pretty impressive appearances around the world. Her animal portraits have been used by Chelsea Textiles (London, Paris, and New York) in their line of hand-stitched tapestry cushions; they've also appeared on a variety of pet gifts in the U. S. In 2009, she was commissioned to do a group piece for the RSPCA Freedom Food Awards. Last, but certainly not least, she designed the Chinese Year of the Dog commemorative coins for the New Zealand Mint. Each coin in the series featured a different breed – Springer spaniel, black Labrador retriever, bloodhound, husky, Newfoundland, Shar Pei, Borzoi, and St. Bernard—and all but three have completely sold out.

"I can draw dogs with my eyes closed!" exclaims Logue. Her first "commissioned" dog portrait was, she adds, for her future husband: "when we first met 20 years ago, he gave me an empty picture frame and asked me to draw something to fill it! If I hadn't drawn his dog, who knows which direction my artwork would have taken me?" So, in that respect, she considers her husband her "biggest influence." Another influence is British artist Lucian Freud (1922 - 2011), who included animals in much of his work. She's particularly drawn to his "Double Portrait" (1985 -86), which features "a woman curled up with her dog. I love the way he uses color to describe the translucence of skin and the way the dog is always the calming element in his painting."

Dogs do make up the bulk of her commissions, followed by horses and cats. But birds, rabbits, sheep, pigs, and other farm animals find their way into her work as well. For the Freedom Food piece, she had to paint "12 farmed animal types, including cattle, sheep, pigs, a duck, a turkey, and a chicken." And a salmon. "You won't believe how hard I had to persuade them to have the salmon drawn separately from the other farmed animals!" Logue laughs. "Farmed salmon don't jump unless stressed, so it had to appear to be happily swimming somewhere in the picture. I have to say, I was surprisingly pleased with the result."

She's not just an animal portraitist, however. In fact, she loves drawing people, "especially if the photo is full of life." One of Logue's favorite people portraits is that of her brother and his wife: "I just love the way Tom is pretending not to enjoy being romantically kissed on the cheek. When you know someone well, it's easier to get a good likeness." She gave the piece to them at their wedding reception and told them it was a mirror. Which, in a sense, you might say it was.

Logue can't really call to mind a time when this passion for art wasn't a part of what she was all about. One of her earliest memories is of "getting a paint box with lots of wonderful colored blocks. I remember being asked if I would like a paint box or a new dress for Christmas. I think I chose the paint box but ended up with both!" And years later, her very first art homework assignment in secondary school "was to draw a pet! I didn't have one at the time – in those days, we didn't even have a picture of a dog in the house – so I had to make it up based on our neighbor's dog." The result—and she still has the sketch book to prove it—was "basically a hairy rectangle with a head and legs" that earned her a "7/10. I knew I could have done better with a reference source, and from then on, I strived to get 10/10 for my art homeworks." You can see that same striving in her work today.

She has also made good the early lack of animal companions with "dogs and cats all my adult life." And the love of that life is Roxy, a Lab-collie cross who came to them from the local animal rescue seven years ago. "Roxy and I enjoy long walks together," Logue enthuses. "She's so responsive and quick to learn. She listens to every word, waiting for the ones she understands! I never need to raise my voice to her, she looks so apologetic if she succumbs to temptation and 'accidentally' empties a bin. And we curl up together, just like the Lucian Freud painting."

Related link:

■ http://www.portraits4pets.com

THE BEST CURMUDGEON EVER:
CLEVELAND AMORY

I FIRST SAW HIM when I was in the 4th grade. My brother Craig had just gotten some literature from the newly formed Fund for Animals; and there, in the brochure, was a photo of its founder and president, Cleveland Amory, standing tall and speaking out for the rights of mustangs, seals, and all other creatures who couldn't speak for themselves. My imagination was fired: that summer, one of my entries in the local 4-H Fair was what I thought of as my "animal conservation scrapbook" with pictures of buffaloes blithely scissored out of an out-of-print history book and literature from the Fund that I'd pilfered from my brother.

Years later, I came across Cleveland Amory's *The Cat Who Came for Christmas*, *The Cat and the Curmudgeon*, and *The Best Cat Ever*. I devoured those books, crying at the end of the third one, when Polar Bear, the curmudgeonly stray who'd taken the activist under his paw, died. Some people complained about that last book – Amory went off on tangents, dropped names, yada yada—but I loved the tangents. They were vivid and peppered with his unmistakable brand of humor. If good writing is, as one of my teachers used to say, like "extraordinarily good talk" – well, Mr. Amory could talk my ear off in print anytime. I never took much stock in the name-dropping charge either. The man simply struck me as being someone with interesting stories to tell, and it just so happened that given the circles he'd traveled in, a lot of famous folks figured in those stories.

So, when my *Just Cats!* Editors, Nancy and Bob Hungerford, told me to go ahead and set up an interview with him, I was delighted. And scared. I mean, this was Cleveland Amory, published author and former *T. V. Guide* critic, I'd be interviewing, a man who was capable of tossing off a verbal barb as lightly and easily as a paper airplane. Then, one Sunday shortly before our scheduled interview, I found myself driving behind a ranger with the word "Curmudgeon" embroidered on its spare-tire cover. I laughed aloud: suddenly, I knew the interview was going to turn out all right.

It turned out more than all right. Cleveland Amory was surprisingly easy to talk to. At one point, he frankly admitted that in the beginning, the term "animals' rights" had made him nervous. "Everything having to do with rights back then," Cleveland explained, "had to do with blacks, more so than women . . . and it seemed to me that saying, 'Animals have rights' might be construed as being disparaging to blacks, and, after all, blacks controlled a lot of animals in Africa and elsewhere."

"I've always preferred the term 'animal conservation,'" I remarked.

"I disagree with you there," he shot back, explaining that the older term focused on wild animals and more or less left the domestic ones out in the cold. Was I smarting from his friendly but firm rebuke? Hell, no. I was exhilarated. It was one of those magical journalistic moments: the interview had stopped being an interview and become a dialogue. I went on to ask him about his personal philosophy, which was, like the man himself, direct and unpretentious. "Simply to be kind," he replied promptly. "That would solve so much."

If our first interview was a Bill Moyers-eque exchange, the second one was like a talk with an old friend. "I love the stuff you sent me," Cleveland told me, referring to my review of *The Best Cat Ever* and a few other things I'd sent him in the interim. "I think they're terrific . . . . You write beautifully."

We talked about the Polar Bear books, and I ran one of his comments by him, hoping to draw some more quotes from him. "Now, the last time we talked," I began, "you said you were trying to get people to see Polar Bear as he was to you."

There was silence on the other end of the line. "That's good," Cleveland finally said. "That's better than anything I could have come up with, except when I was younger."

We talked about the cat novel for young adults I'd just finished (*Houdini*) and – briefly – about the book he was premeditating (*Ranch of Dreams,* as it turned out). "You're going to write that," he retorted. Chuckling, he repeated, "You're going to write it. I'm the senior writer – I've been working in the goddamn trenches long enough." Shortly after that, he remarked, "You know, I'm sick of talking to you on the phone. Come down to the office here sometime."

So, early that November, I walked into the Fund's office. Cleveland looked up and gestured to the wide windowsill to the right of his desk. I hopped up and took out my ice-cream-sandwich-sized tape recorder, only to discover that the batteries had died in transit. I tossed the tape recorder back into my bag and whipped out my steno pad and pen.

We ended up spending over an hour together – partly putting the finishing touches on our interview, partly just visiting. Actually, we did more of the latter. One of Cleveland's strengths was, I think, that he didn't stand on ceremony. This lion was comfortable enough with himself that he didn't have to. Roar, that is. Not about silly formalities. No, he was going to save his roars for what really mattered: his work on behalf of the animals.

He was a generous-hearted lion, too – generous with his time and with his praise. As we chatted, he'd toss off a friendly remark: "You should be reviewing all this – You're funny – We think alike." As I rose to leave, he took the *Houdini* manuscript from me, glanced at it, and said, "I know this'll be good." He asked me if I had an agent. When I replied that I didn't, Cleveland replied, "Well, I think an agent would be very interested in you. Some people are only one-book writers – you're not. You're going to be writing for the rest of your life." And he autographed the copy of *The Best Cat Ever* that I'd brought along with me: "For T. J. It was a pleasure being interviewed by a writer I know who is just at the dawn of a fine career. Cleveland Amory. Nov. 7, 1994."

He sat back and eyed what he'd written. "Hmmph," he said matter-of-factly. "Looks like 'damn.'" And it did. He handed me back the book, and we shook hands. 'Call any time," he told me. I left his office a-glow. It didn't matter whether anything more came of this – it didn't even really matter whether I heard from him again. What *did* matter was that that someone who mattered as a writer thought that I did, too.

But I did hear from him a few weeks later, and his response to *Houdini* was all a writer could ask for:

" . . . I thoroughly enjoyed Houdini. What a sweet, loyal soul. And what a brave one, to boot.

"Now, mind you, I am a few years older than your target audience. But only a few. So I can safely say you have a winner on your hands." He went on to make a suggestion regarding one of my secondary characters, then concluded, *"Meanwhile, I hope other people like Houdini as much as I – and I look forward to seeing it in bookstores before long. Be sure and let me know your progress. By the way, do you want your manuscript back?*

"With warmest wishes,
Cleveland Amory."

We corresponded fairly regularly after that. He always responded in a warm, friendly fashion to whatever writing news I shared with him, suggesting what he felt was a better title for one of my essays or laughing off a typo in my published interview with him. "A piece of journalism as positive as *Making a difference . . .* can," he observed dryly, "can afford one 'Amry.'"

Then, on July 11, 1995, my husband, Tim, was killed in a freak car accident coming home, and Cleveland's response showed that he more than lived up to his philosophy of "simply to be kind":

"Your letter was waiting for me upon my return from a long trip. What can I say?

"'Sorry' is such an insignificant little word. Yet I do want you to know how sad I am for you. I am also gratified that you were able to take solace from the last chapter of The Best Cat Ever. *You are quite right. Tim would most assuredly not quibble over a cat/human distinction.*

"I enjoyed your 'Out-of-Print Cat Books' article and, of course, I am terribly pleased over the acceptance from Poets & Writers *– though I understand full well how this lacks the thrill it might have once had for you.*

"In closing, let me add my hopes that with each passing day, you will feel a little better. It goes without saying but if there is anything I can do to help, please do not hesitate to ask."

We met again at the Fund's office that Halloween. As usual, Cleveland was down-to-earth and to-the-point. We talked about everything from Tim, our daughter Marissa, and the cats-in-residence to what I was currently working on ("You have a sense of humor," he remarked approvingly, "and it shows in your writing.") and finding an agent for *Houdini*. He took a few minutes out then and there to place phone calls to his various contacts for me, leaving messages like "This is the IRS. Why aren't you at your desk? I can't stand this type of dereliction . . . ." He never left his name, but that voice with its Bostonian accent was unmistakable. Besides, I had a pretty strong hunch that the folks who knew Cleveland were used to finding messages like that on their answering machines.

There is one memory-picture from that visit that still makes me smile. At some point during our chat, the phone rang, and Cleveland excused himself to take the call. He didn't say much, just started chuckling. "Marian!" he suddenly bellowed. "Marian! Come in here and listen to what Ed has to say about his desk!"

There was an ominous silence. Then Marian Probst, his long-time secretary and the Fund's treasurer "under whose incredible memory for irritating facts he [the author] has, with the patience of Job, long suffered" (*The Cat and the Curmudgeon*), marched into his office. "Cleveland," she said shortly, "I was on the phone about greyhound racing. I could not come and listen to what Ed has to say about his desk." And turned out her heel and marched out.

Cleveland sat there quietly for a moment. Then his desire to share the joke got the better of him, and he turned to me. "Ed's this lawyer," he explained. "Very funny guy. Anyway, someone came in to talk to him, looked at his desk, and said, 'Were there any survivors?'" He chuckled again, shaking his head ruefully. "A writer would have given anything to come up with that . . . ."

The other thing I remember vividly is the book-signing. This time, I'd brought the first two books in the Polar Bear trilogy with me. Cleveland took them and scribbled away for a few minutes, pausing only to ask me our cats' names or to check the spelling of Marissa's ("Because, of course, she's going to read these some day," he told me.); then he handed them back to me, saying, "There! I've signed my name, so you can't give 'em away."

I flipped open *The Cat Who Came for Christmas*. On the title page, he'd written, "For TJ and Cricket and Kilah and Dervish and Tikvah and Zorro and Woody and Boris and Starfire – and of course Marissa. With love to you all, Cleveland." But it was the inscription in *The Cat and the Curmudgeon* that really caught me by the throat: "For TJ and Marissa and in memory of Tim – with special affection – Cleveland Amory."

I looked up at Cleveland. "He would have been pleased," I said softly. And that one gesture on his part convinced me more than anything else that Cleveland Amory was a class act.

We continued our correspondence. Sometimes it would be awhile before I heard from Cleveland – there were book tours and, of course, business for the Fund – but he never failed to respond. "I am also pleased over the spirit of your letter," he wrote shortly after our meeting, "—it seemed much lighter, almost back to the way things were when I first met you. Hopefully, this is a reflection of your true feelings." Or, after those first holidays without Tim: "I thought about you during the Christmas holidays, knowing this was yet another thing to be 'gotten through.' But I see by your letter you have come through with flying colors. Not that I doubted you would. But it is nice to have it confirmed." And the condolence note he wrote me after my favorite cat Cricket's death was just as thoughtful as the one he'd written me after Tim's: "Not only do I feel for you but know only too well what you are feeling. *The Best Bet,* [my essay about Cricket,] however, is a lovely tribute to her."

There were lighter notes, too, such as when I thought I'd landed a publisher for my novel: "Three cheers, and then some, over the happy news about *Houdini.* Really, I could not be more pleased and eagerly await my copy. Inscribed, please." Or when one of my essays had been picked up for *Chocolate for a Woman's Heart:* "So here I am again with kudos . . . even if their title is indeed inferior. This from someone who is quite partial to chocolates."

We had a brief chat in April 1998, when the *Houdini* contract fell through. Cleveland was warm and affectionate, assuring me that the publishers had to give me my manuscript back. Then, before he signed off, he said, "By the way, Sally here was asking how you were doing." I honestly didn't remember who Sally was – I must've met her in passing during one of my visits – but it was such a typically down-to-earth homey Cleveland-ish statement. It was also one of the last things I ever heard him say.

I didn't hear about his death till the Friday after it happened. A few days later, Barbara Bowen of Bowen Books sent me a copy of Cleveland's obit from *The New York Post*. "What a grand and full life he had," she wrote simply. To me, that was the best – the most fitting – epitaph ever. No living in half-shadows, no simply going through the motions for Cleveland Amory. He had lived his life grandly, fully, no-holds-barred. And how glad I was to have shared a few moments of that life with him.

Not long afterwards, I was working on a crossword puzzle and happened upon the following clue: "Conservationist Cleveland." Immediately, my mind sped back to that first long-ago interview. I grinned to myself and inked in my "Amry."

Point for my side, Cleveland.